D1594502

THE BIG THING EFFECT

How to Transform Your Life Forever

Jeff Patterson

Published by Aspen Success Press
400 W. Main Street, #204
Aspen CO 81611

Every effort has been made to obtain permissions for material quoted throughout the book. If any required acknowledgements have been omitted, or any rights overlooked, it is unintentional. Please notify the publisher of any omission, and it will be rectified in future editions.

Author's Note: Where I've used first and last names, these are clients who have given permission to include them. Otherwise, I've changed the client's name and identifying details to protect their privacy.

ISBN 979-8-9863674-0-8
Library of Congress Control Number: 2022912477

Cover design by: Jerry Todd
Interior design and formatting by Alyssa Ohnmacht
Printed in the United States

What Readers Are Saying

"As an athlete I know the value of having a coach. But words cannot express the value of coaching that brings out the best in you. My coaching with Jeff Patterson has been life changing. His instincts and ability to hone in on things you can't even see is remarkable. Jeff's coaching has made me a better sports analyst and commentator, it's assisted me to stretch and serve more in my business and philanthropic pursuits. Most importantly it's challenging me to go even farther than I thought was possible in all areas of my life."

~ Chris Evert,
Tennis Champion

"Wow! This is truly epic! *The Big Thing Effect* is like a personal conversation with Jeff—deeply inspiring and will ignite you to go *all in* for your best life. It reads like an adventure thriller while teaching and inspiring you every step of the way. This is medicine for your soul ... A must read!"

~ Darin Olien,
#1 *New York Times* bestselling author of *Superlife,*
Co-host of Netflix *"Down To Earth* with Zac Efron"

"As a founder and CEO, I am always looking for ways to learn, grow and elevate my performance. I am a voracious reader and reading *The Big Thing Effect* sparked many new insights that I'm already applying ... and it's making a powerful impact. Jeff's honest account of his own challenges and lessons made this book extremely relatable. I've experienced his powerful coaching but this book opened my eyes to even more. I highly recommend this book!"

~ Troy Swope,
Co-founder and CEO of Footprint

"What a great book. It challenges readers to dare to let go of the unreal beliefs that lock them in a relatively small game of life. Those who are successful in creating their 'Big Thing' are now ready to explore the amazing opportunity of what their 'Real You' is destined to do."

~ Ron Hulnick, co-author with Mary Hulnick,
Loyalty to Your Soul: The Heart of Spiritual Psychology

"This book literally changed my life. Instantly. Written with such authenticity, great personal vulnerability, raw wisdom, and laugh-out-loud storytelling, I didn't want to put it down. I learned creative and simple tools to become aware of character traits that hijacked my energy and motivation. The exercises got me to the root of my challenges, and showed how to have the courage to make positive and supportive changes in my life without changing others!"

~ Tara Sheahan, Founder,
Conscious Global Leadership

Table of Contents

Prologue: Stuck in the Clouds   **1**

**Introduction: What Would You Dare to Do or
"Die Trying"?**   **7**
Metaphorical Death   9
What's Stopping You: Small Vision Syndrome   10
Your Big Thing   11

Chapter 1: Hear the Call of Your Big Thing   **17**
Seven Signposts That Tell You It's a Big Thing   23
Possible is a State of Mind   27
A Big Goal vs. A Big Thing   31

Chapter 2: Know You Are More Than You Think   **35**
Unlock the Gamechanger in You   38
The Essential Self vs. The Conditioned Self   39
We Become our Identity   46

Chapter 3: Clarify Your Vision   **51**
The Power of Visualizing Your Future   54
When the Vision is Clear the Resources Appear   58
When It's Written It's Real   63

Chapter 4: Decide, Declare... Then Fully Commit   **79**
Intention vs Commitment   84
Self-Created Urgency   88
Inner Commitment   97

Chapter 5: Focus on the Moment   **99**

   Think Small to Go Big   105

   Remove Distractions   106

   Getting Comfortable with Discomfort   113

Chapter 6: Shift Your Way of Being   **117**

   Who Are You Being?   120

   We Create from the Level of Being   127

   Being a Champion Precedes Winning a Championship   129

Chapter 7: Turn Obstacles into Opportunities   **141**

   Your Big Thing Will Reveal What's Holding You Back   147

   Don't Let Your "Story" Stop You   149

   Pain is Inevitable. Suffering is Optional   152

Chapter 8: Use It All to Serve   **155**

   Contribution as a Motivator   159

   BYOB: Be Your Own Bestie   162

   Use Your Intuition   170

Chapter 9: Let Go of the Guarantee   **173**

   Certainty in Place of Confidence   176

   Tapping Out   177

Chapter 10: "Die Trying"   **179**

Chapter 11: The Return   **185**

   Coming Home   188

   No Holding Back   190

Chapter 12: Are You Ready for the Climb of Your Life?   **191**

Acknowledgments   **195**

About the Author   **197**

A Special Invitation   **198**

For my dad, Al Patterson,
who taught me
the life-changing power
of a Big Thing.

PROLOGUE

Stuck in the Clouds

Day 12 • February 1, 2011
Aconcagua High Camp 3, Plaza Cólera • 19,200 feet

At 4:01 a.m. everything goes quiet, like someone flipped a switch. The silence is deafening. For the past thirty-six hours, wind and snow has been assaulting our tents and we've been hunkered down, waiting for the weather to break. Seventy mile per hour winds drove temperatures to thirty below. I've slept a total of ten hours over the past fourteen nights while fighting intense altitude sickness. We're in Western Argentina on Plaza Cólera, High Camp, 19,200 feet up the south side of Mt. Aconcagua—the Mt. Everest of the Western hemisphere, and one of the "Seven Summits." Over the last two weeks, our original climbing team of ten has dwindled to seven. Two had to bail, and one of our three guides went to escort them down the mountain.

The hiss of a stove in our climbing guides' tent breaks the silence. That can mean only one thing. We're going for the summit. My next thought is, *Oh, shit!* I was secretly hoping the wind would give us another day or two of rest, but the weather window is here. Ready or not, it's time to make our bid for the summit. I slither out of the tent and start suiting up.

My appetite is gone, but I know I must eat. We have more than 3,600 feet to climb and I'm running on fumes. I pull breakfast from my pocket—a slab of vanilla poundcake. It was moist when we started. Now it's a dusty rock entombed in Saran. The thought of even one bite turns my stomach, but I break off a piece and stuff it into my dry mouth, washing it down with water that smells of iodine.

We huddle together in the black velvet of predawn, staring up into a sea of stars, but there's no time to relish the beauty. We must press ahead because time is precious.

The team is moving quickly, but I struggle to keep pace. As we continue up the mountain, the wind is picking up. I wipe the snow from my goggles and can now see the most dangerous part of the climb, the Windy Traverse, a foot-wide ridge pitched at 45-degrees, with a 1,000-foot drop off to the right. We must walk this narrow path for a quarter mile with no margin for error.

The altitude sickness is gripping my head like a vise, and nausea has me regretting the pound cake. Each second of the climb becomes more arduous than the last, and my resolve is starting to weaken. As my teammates and the lead guide surge ahead, the distance between us widens. I feel alone and defeated and deeply ashamed for not keeping up. More than a year of training has led up to this, and I seriously fear I will not reach the summit.

What kind of team leaves you behind like this? I wonder, slipping into a victim story. The angry voice in my head then turns on me. *You'll never make it. What were you thinking? You're not ready for this! You'll get hurt. Or worse.* I begin to obsess on the fact that Mt. Aconcagua has the highest death rate of any mountain in South America—more than 100 since records began—earning the nickname, "Mountain of Death."

I lean on my ice axe, dizzy and off-balance, struggling to breathe. Just before I enter the traverse, several climbers from a German team pass ahead of me, including a 50-year-old man wearing a red down suit. The embarrassment only deepens. My fingers and toes, already throbbing from the cold, are losing sensation. Frostbite is a real risk. I bang my boots against each other and slap my gloved hands to get some circulation going. Nothing is working.

By now, the rest of the team is at least a mile ahead and 1,000 feet above. I can no longer see them as I fall back another twenty feet behind the German, his red suit, thank God, still visible through the blowing snow. He enters the traverse and I'm intent on keeping him in sight. I tell myself, *if I can just keep pace with him, I'll make it.* He becomes my beacon, my secret climbing buddy. I'm no longer alone.

We climb on for a few more minutes when suddenly, his balance wavers. The next few seconds unfold in surreal slow motion as he snags a crampon on his pants, stumbles, then trips forward, bouncing against a rock, and tumbles over the edge like a ragdoll until he slams onto the ice, 1,000 feet below. I press my back and outstretched arms against a boulder and hold my breath, staring at his motionless body far below. I snap my eyelids up and down trying to wake from this nightmare. My brain is starved of food, oxygen and sleep. As I look down at him, I see myself. I witness my unlived life, my unrealized dreams, and all the potential that has not yet been realized. I've never felt so small, insignificant, and alone. My knees wobble as the last shred of confidence and strength drains away. There's so much I haven't done, so much I haven't fully expressed. Have I become who I came here to *be*? Have I done what I came here to do? The answer is a resounding *NO!!!!!*

Fixated on the fallen climber, I'm frozen in my tracks, tears fogging my goggles. *What do I do? Continue or retreat?* The voice in my head screams, *what the hell were you thinking? You have no business being here! You're gonna **die** on this mountain, die on this mountain, die on this mountain…*

INTRODUCTION:

What Would You Dare to Do or "Die Trying"?

WHAT WOULD YOU DARE TO DO
OR "DIE TRYING"?

Does this question stop your breath and quicken your pulse? If so, read on, because this is the conversation I want to have with you. It has the power to transform your life forever.

The words "die trying" are radical. Of course, you wouldn't want to intentionally do anything that would end your life. Even so, this question has the potential to unlock something sleeping deep within you. As you explore this question, you may feel anxiety in your chest. You'll want to get up out of your seat and get something to eat, or use the restroom, or do just about *anything* other than think about this. Yet, you will also feel something else as well: *your alive-ness.* Nudging your attention toward the subject of dying has you experiencing the palpable reality that you are, in fact, *living.*

What exactly does "die trying" mean? It's that thing you'd be metaphorically willing to die for because, if you *don't* do it, you'll be dead *inside.* This is not necessarily something that's so dangerous it would put your life in peril. In many cases, the thing someone wants to do *is* important enough to die for, but it doesn't necessarily involve risk of physical death.

Metaphorical Death
Metaphorical death is really the death of the ego, the end of the stories you tell about yourself. Are you willing to break the chains, and let go of the trappings that hold you back? Are you

willing to say "yes" to something your heart and soul are calling you to do? As long as you listen to that fearful voice, you'll never hear the quiet whispers calling you.

Exploring what you'd dare to do or die trying will nudge you toward the release of:

- The idea of *security*
- Distraction from what's most important
- Others' ideas of who you *should* be
- The part of you that *pleases* rather than lives fully
- Holding back and making *excuses*
- Avoiding the unpleasant *work*
- Blocks that have previously held you back

What's Stopping You: Small Vision Syndrome

Most people are not *really* living. Ask yourself, are you truly living your most authentic and full-throttle life? Are you pursuing endeavors that are deeply meaningful? Are you making a difference? Are you growing? Are you living fully? Are you being the person you most want to be? This is not the time to fool yourself and accept anything less than your genuine, deep truth. Even if you're living a good life, your answer may be "no."

There's a malady that has wormed its way into the psyche of modern humanity. It's the affliction of avoiding discomfort. Aversion to risk has lulled even the brightest into thinking small. It seems harmless enough, even wise: *If I don't think I can reach a goal, then why set myself up for disappointment?* Our environment reinforces this story until it becomes conditioned. A person can become cemented in their habitual tendency to avoid what's most important. This is Small Vision Syndrome.

This syndrome is the byproduct of focusing more on your circumstances and fears than on your dreams and possibilities. Make no mistake, Small Vision Syndrome (SVS) is dangerous. It can take your life. Not your physical life, but the inner life that's yearning to come out. Day-by-day, it slowly sucks away your motivation, strength, and energy. It's a death by a thousand cuts. It will rob you of the resources you'll need most to realize your biggest goals and dreams.

Why are we moved to tears when we watch a talented actor deliver the performance of a lifetime, or a skilled athlete do the impossible? It's because we feel that it takes epic soul to deliver such an outcome. Yet we often doubt this greatness in ourselves. We can even get caught up in watching others soar rather than strapping on wings and flying. We watch our favorite team on TV and jump up off the couch and proclaim, "We won!" No, *you* didn't win anything. You watched while someone *else* won. There's a difference.

I believe every one of us is here to leave our unique mark on the world—to be agents of change, using our gifts to make the world a better place. I also believe that many of us have given up on our dreams and parked our aspirations behind the responsibilities of everyday living. While this is, unfortunately, common, it doesn't have to be that way.

I discovered SVS when I noticed my own backing off from *my* dreams as a transformational success coach, expert speaker, and author. More than once, I had to name this behavior so I could see it, then start to do something about it.

If you're not willing to admit that you suffer from this affliction, then you're not free to choose something else. No one is immune to SVS, regardless of your previous level of accomplishment. There's no vaccine, but there is a cure: your Big Thing.

Your Big Thing

Your Big Thing is something *big*. You know. *That* thing. It's the thing you've been thinking about doing for years, but you may not dare to say it aloud. You'll know if it's your Big Thing because, when you think about it, your breath may stop, your pulse may quicken, and your stomach may drop, because doing a Big Thing is scary. It's *so* big you're not sure *how*, or even *if*, it can get done. It's bigger than you. It will require miracles to materialize. It will require something of you, and you may not have a clue what that something will be.

While you might have been thinking about your Big Thing for decades, you also might not yet consciously know what it is, but you can feel it. Something is tugging at you, telling you that you have unrealized potential, and if you bring it forward and express it, a new world will be possible.

Your Big Thing is an endeavor that calls out to your heart, mind, and soul. It draws on *all* of you, because it will *take* all of you, and more, to pursue and sustain it. When I say "big," I mean it's big for *you*, and, as you'll learn in the pages that follow, sometimes a Big Thing can start small. The "big" nature of a Big Thing is that it's deeply important to *you*, and not necessarily large in a worldly scope. It's not "big for the sake of big."

This is not about an unhealthy validation of insecurity or ego gratification. Rather, a Big Thing is about honoring the deeply compelling nature of what's seeking to emerge from within. It's about having the courage to follow and create it, even though it may be scary.

Your Big Thing is about saying "yes" to the biggest, most important endeavor of your life at this time. It will make you grow, and reveal from within a wilder, brighter, and bigger self that has been buried under those old habits of thinking that have kept you playing small.

Ask yourself, "What's that thing, the BIG THING," you want to do, that you may never have spoken of aloud?

I've been posing this question to people for the past four decades. It's helped me create a special bond with people. When they start to think about and share their deepest desires, something is set loose in their lives. Their eyes light up and they begin to see new possibilities.

If you're not clear, that's fine; that's the point. How often do you slow down to actually contemplate this? The day-to-day tasks of living gobble up so much energy that there's little left for such consideration. Even if you're clear about your Big Thing, it's easy to avoid in favor of the daily grind. This is a travesty. We're not living to merely get stuff done. We're here to *thrive*, and you can't thrive if your focus is only on the To-Do list.

Some people have a "Bucket List." Your Big Thing might be on it. It might be at the top. More likely, it's near the bottom. So, consider what is *the* thing you know you must do before this life is over? That thing you *came here to do*? Or the thing that you know, deep down, you'll regret not having done?

I'm often asked, "Do we have just *one* Big Thing in life"? No, but you only have one Big Thing *at a time*. The *next* Big Thing. The one that's calling you most right now. And sometimes, you might be inspired to do a Big Thing that will prepare you so that you're ready to do an even *bigger* Big Thing on the other side, something you couldn't possibly do yet because of Small Vision Syndrome. There's an experience you need to have that will forge you and transform you into who you need to be.

But either way, when you finally stop and listen, you'll realize that there's a Big Thing in you, wanting to come out.

The Big Thing Effect

"When you go for your
Big Thing, magic happens.
It puts you in touch with the deeper realms
of being that you're thirsting for."

The exciting impact is that those qualities will immediately begin pulsing through your being. This "aliveness" starts affecting everything you do.

Many people love foreign travel for similar reasons. You never knew what challenges you might face, yet the adversity reveals hidden resilience. Breaking routine shakes you out of your automatic responses, to be more present to the experience. This makes you feel alive and energized, and stimulates your creativity in ways that everyday living may not. This surge in power and aliveness starts pouring out into all the other areas of your life, without even thinking about it. In some cases, this blast of energy can overcome challenges that previously seemed impossible.

The Seven Keys to Doing Your Big Thing

In *The Big Thing Effect*, you will learn seven keys, or principles, that when applied together, will help you obliterate Small Vision Syndrome and realize your Big Thing. These keys will also release the brightest, boldest, and most authentic version of yourself, and change your life forever. They are:

1. Know you are more than you think
2. Clarify your vision
3. Decide and declare . . . then fully commit
4. Focus on the moment
5. Shift your way of being
6. Turn obstacles into opportunities
7. Use it all to serve

The Invitation: Let the Tiger Out of the Cage

I'm honored that you're here. The information and true stories you're about to read are the culmination of more than twenty years of coaching clients to ignite unprecedented levels of aliveness and impact. You'll read about my personal journey of heartbreak, loss, and triumph on one of the world's highest mountains. You will also uncover insights from the many inspiring people I've had the privilege of coaching, but most of all, this book is about *you*.

While I share many personal stories, the deeper intention is to help you access your own stories and wisdom. As you read, stay connected to what is coming up inside of yourself, especially your insights. Doing this will make the stories, examples, and principles come to life in a very personal way.

There are two ways you can read the contents. You can either get information or create transformation. I encourage you to do the latter. If you're only looking for information, you'll miss a deeper opportunity. Give yourself permission to read at your own pace. Grab a journal and write down insights and questions as you read and you'll walk away with more than ideas. You'll leave with an experience that has the power to revolutionize your life forever.

You're not here by accident. If you've read this far, I know there's something meaningful trying to emerge from within you. It's more than just a goal. It's a part of you that's longing to be fully expressed, a part deep down waiting for the opportunity to pounce on life. Many of us have lived our lives like tigers in a cage, pacing back and forth, waiting for that mythic *someday* when someone or something will come along and open it up, and we can finally escape to be the person we most want to be.

The Big Thing Effect is your invitation to open that cage.

To set the tiger free, take on your Big Thing and radically embrace all of who you truly are, right now. And rather than hide it, judge it, or alter it, boldly share it in the world in your own unique way, without apology. No more waiting. No more wishing.

It's time to stop trying to find yourself and begin *unlocking* yourself. You don't need to compare, or attempt to be like anyone else. This is not about developing a persona, or acting "as if" you were someone else. The person you want to be, and so much more, is alive deep down inside you.

What would it take for you to be the person you *truly* are, the person you were *born* to be, no matter where you currently are in your life, what you own, or what others say?

You don't need another cent in your bank account to do that. You don't need another degree to unleash your brilliance, and you don't need more time to become who you most want to be. All you need is the courage to share your deepest, most honest self, and share it in service to others. This will have you tapping into a wellspring of aliveness that will have people gathering around you like moths, attracted by your flame.

My challenge to you is this: pursue the question, what's your Big Thing? And not only to *answer* it, but then to *do* it. Take on the climb of your life, a climb that will take you beyond your own limits and have you feeling radically alive. This is an aliveness that money can't buy, people can't steal, and the market cannot discount. This is a power that moves mountains, and has people doing what others say can't be done.

If you're ready, I'm here to lead, and climb with you all the way to the summit. Let's do this!

CHAPTER 1

Hear the Call of Your Big Thing

THE INVITATION

May 10, 2010 • Grays Peak, Colorado • 14,000 feet

In May of 2010, I climbed my first fourteener, Grays Peak, the tenth-highest summit of the Rocky Mountains of North America. Grays is also one of the easiest of all the 14,000 foot-plus peaks in Colorado.

We left the trailhead around 9:00 a.m. and reached the summit by noon. A pair of mountain goats stared at us like we had invaded their living room. Despite a nagging knee, I made it to the top. It was thrilling.

"This is incredible!" I shouted. We could see 100 miles in every direction. I'd always dreamed of climbing mountains, living an adventurous life, but for some time I'd been feeling stuck and frustrated. I'd been gaining some ground in my business, but still kept playing small, getting caught up in my own limiting behavior. I had big aspirations of coaching individuals of significant influence and impact, writing books, and inspiring audiences around the country. Yet it seemed far off in the distance. Though my coaching business was beginning to thrive, I was so focused on building the business day-to-day, that the larger vision seemed too lofty to think about, and I wasn't really progressing on that larger vision.

Standing there, bathed in dazzling high-altitude sunshine, Stephen McGhee, my business coach at the time, asked me, "Are you truly committed to creating a change in your business?"

Gazing out at the far horizons, I said, "Yes! Absolutely."

"Well then, I'd invite you to consider joining me on an expedition to climb Mt. Aconcagua." He proposed that I join him and five other men to train for eight months, then travel to Argentina and spend up to a month climbing the 22,841-foot mountain. Mt. Aconcagua is one of the infamous "Seven Summits." It's the highest mountain in South America and the highest mountain in the world outside of Asia.

"Really? You think I could actually do that?" At first, I was honored that he considered me a candidate. Then fear set in, and I could only see the barriers. I thought, *Are you kidding? I'm not that guy. I'm not ready for that kind of adventure.*

"How much would it cost?" I heard myself ask tentatively, despite my aversion to the idea.

"Fifty thousand, all in," he said, "including the trip, training, and a year of personal coaching."

What? No way! I could barely pay the rent, and between school loans and credit card debt, I still owed $60,000. Fifty grand was *twice* my income from the previous year. I didn't have the money to buy gear, flights, and travel, let alone accommodation and guide fees. I'd be away from my business for a month. How in the world would I pay for a trip like this?

Even if I could afford it, the timing was not ideal. My girlfriend Lindsay and I had just purchased a small home to remodel. This added to the financial stress and also demanded a lot of physical work. I'd never taken on a remodel, and had no clue what I was getting into. Certainly, there was no sane reason to add another big project on top of that! How would I manage this along with growing my business and training for such a momentous (and dangerous) climb? It obviously was not the right time.

But an even bigger obstacle loomed. I was deathly afraid of heights. I mean *terrified*. Two years prior in California, on my second date with Lindsay, we were doing a ropes course. I climbed a ladder four feet up a redwood toward a forty-foot platform, and I froze. I couldn't move, and my eyes welled up with tears. I felt like a complete wuss.

Well, if I'm able to climb Grays Peak…, I thought, as I contemplated Stephen's invitation, but then realized that a six-hour day hike was a walk in the park compared to nearly twenty days on a mountain that is 8,000 feet higher.

Despite being unable to see how it was possible, I was excited by the idea, and Stephen encouraged me to take some time to consider it.

Over the next two weeks, I tortured myself, flip flopping back and forth like a trout on the dock, gasping for air, trying to decide whether or not I should commit.

How do I really know if I'm ready? I *wanted* to be ready, but was I? *What if I got injured, or worse?* If this were right for me, surely I wouldn't be so fraught with doubt. This expedition couldn't be a wise choice.

At the core of my conflict, deep down was a feeling that I wasn't ready for a challenge this big. In short, I was suffering from Small Vision Syndrome. This was the *real* reason I was holding back. Who was I to go for something this big? *Yes,* I wanted to do it. *Yes,* it had benefits, but it felt decadent—a luxury I had not yet earned the right to enjoy.

I hated this internal response. It felt so limiting. After all, as a coach, I challenged people every day to face their fears and do the thing they most want to do, despite the odds. My hesitation exposed a crack in my armor, a place where I was not being the man I truly wanted to be. I was being a man who had great potential, but didn't have the ability or the right to go *that* big yet. This thinking went against everything I challenged other people to do. I could feel the integrity gap. It only added fuel to the fire of this very uncomfortable decision.

Frustrated, I started to talk to this part of myself. *You don't think I can do this?*

It sharply responded, *Hell no! I don't think you* can, *nor that you should! You have so much work to do before you go off somewhere and play in the mountains. It's irresponsible. Not only that, this is a ridiculous conversation given your terror of heights! And it doesn't matter because you can't afford it.*

21

This rationale was all too familiar. Any time I wanted something I didn't think I could afford, this was the voice that interrupted. It was uncomfortable and downright debilitating, like Mom telling my best friend, "No, he can't come out to play." Yet, it was *me* saying it.

I felt defeated and shameful. Here I was in my late thirties, and still in this position where I couldn't afford something bold like this. I should be farther along. I was judging myself for where I was in life.

I also falsely believed I couldn't rise above it. You might say I had forgotten who I really was. I was stuck in a limited, small-minded identity, one of the debilitating side effects of Small Vision Syndrome. It felt heavy. It was a pattern that was ruling me, even though I wasn't aware of it. I'd forgotten that I was powerful and that deep down I was more than this. I couldn't access that part of me because I was so focused on the reasons why I thought I couldn't have it. Small Vision Syndrome had quietly snuck into my life, and particularly into my coaching, so I strived to give this invitation real consideration.

It seemed impossible on so many fronts and it was obvious that I'd have to become someone new if I were actually going to do it, because I couldn't accomplish this feat by being the person I had been. I feared I wouldn't be able to become this different person, but the idea that I *could*, inspired me. I was tired of saying "no." I was tired of believing adventures like this were for others. I wanted to break free. I realized that the simple act of climbing the mountain was not the motivator for me, but the deeper growth that I knew was available.

Saying "yes" to climbing Aconcagua would disrupt my life. This wasn't only an adventure. It required having to become more of the man I said I wanted to be. It would take a massive commitment—perhaps more than I've ever demonstrated. Because this was *so* big, there were things I'd need to learn, and I had no idea what those might even be. This would be very uncomfortable and demand that I sort out parts of my life that were not working, such as my meager earnings and fear of commitment. The pain of working those out might be even more daunting than the expedition.

One night, at 3:00 a.m., I woke up in a cold sweat. I realized even though I was scared, deep down I wanted to climb Aconcagua. It was truly calling me, but then I looked at Lindsay sleeping next to me. I recalled the way she looked at me a few days ago when I'd told her I was considering this.

Her expression all but said, "You're going to risk your life to climb some dumb mountain in South America. ARE YOU NUTS?"

She was right. This was nuts.

Seeking answers, I hopped on the Internet to learn more about Aconcagua. Big mistake. Of those who attempt the climb, only half reach the summit. Even worse, three climbers had died in the past month due to brutally cold temperatures and an avalanche. Feeling totally overwhelmed, I did what any sane human would do. I wrote Stephen an email to tell him no. I just wasn't ready.

I signed my name at the end of the email and sat there watching the cursor blink on the screen for at least five minutes before finally hitting *send*.

Seven Signposts That Tell You It's a Big Thing

A Big Thing calls you from within. Some people may wake up one day with a clear realization, a mission, a vocation. They feel in their bones there's more for them, and they know exactly what it is. Others may stumble upon an opportunity, like I did, that invites them to step up to a new and expanded level. Unfortunately, many never act on it. Instead, they stay stuck in doubt, fear, or habit. This is what was happening to me. I was avoiding the call.

It doesn't matter if you don't know where the call is taking you. What matters is that *you have been called*. Know that considering your Big Thing can be scary. It's also unsettling because your ego hates change. The ego is a person's sense of self-esteem or self-importance. Change means growth, and growth means death to the ego.

But what I remind my clients of, over and over, is that it's usually not the things we've done that we live to regret, but rather the things we didn't do. If you don't clarify your Big Thing—that which you truly and deeply want to do—that which would set your soul on fire, you run the risk of regret.

What's that bigger thing that you're yearning to do? Maybe you've never explored the question. Maybe you've forgotten it. Perhaps you have no idea of what your Big Thing is, yet you have a sense that there's something more. Maybe you do know what your Big Thing is, but think it's too fanciful. Or maybe you've distracted yourself with busyness and achievement and tried to convince yourself that you're living life to the fullest.

No matter where you are in life, there's a Big Thing brewing in you. Everybody has one, and it's essential that you pursue it. The clues are deep down and often so close we don't see them. Sometimes certain desires and forces are bubbling beneath, then an opportunity shows up that catalyzes all of those forces into a Big Thing.

To help you discover your Big Thing, here are seven signposts all Big Things have in common:

1. You deeply want it (heart and soul).
2. It scares you.
3. It may seem impossible.
4. The "how" may (temporarily) elude you.
5. You need help to realize it.
6. You must transform in order to reach it.
7. It will serve others.

1. You deeply want it (heart and soul)

It's connected to the deeper dreams you've held inside. Climbing a big mountain like Aconcagua was something I'd always dreamed of, but this expedition represented something much bigger. It represented living boldly, not letting limitations keep me from what I desired. This endeavor was also tied to a desire to use adventures to greater serve clients in a fun and meaningful way.

A Big Thing is not just a big step. It's not, "I'll ask for a raise," or "I'll finally put up my website." Instead, it's statements like:

"I'm going to take my 18-piece big band to China and be an envoy for peace."

"I'm going to become the philanthropist I've always dreamed of and give a million dollars to charity."

"I'm leaving my career on Wall Street for something more meaningful."

Size alone doesn't mean it's a bona fide Big Thing. I'm not pushing you to make your Big Thing bigger, and this is not necessarily about seeking public acclaim.

Rather, I'm asking you to give yourself permission to want what you truly want, even if it's bigger (or different) than you think you're capable of, or ready for. Have the courage to follow what's calling you. That big desire in your heart is not there by accident. It feels so compelling because it is pursuing you as much as you are pursuing it.

2. It scares you

Because it's big, and because it's so much more than a goal, your Big Thing will kick up fear, doubt, and resistance. It makes you question your sanity for even considering it. Others certainly will. So, you might be thinking, "Why would I intentionally choose to be afraid, uncomfortable, and doubt myself?"

Just because it scares you doesn't mean you shouldn't do it. More importantly, being scared doesn't mean it's not meant for you. In fact, it might be a sign. Fear and excitement *feel* the same. They're a sign that you're alive. But many people avoid their Big Thing because they don't want to trigger those intimidating sensations. People often resist the idea of pursuing their Big Thing because they don't *need* it. They have some level of success or satisfaction; why upset the apple cart? After all, you don't have to do a Big Thing to have a comfortable life.

Let's be clear. A Big Thing will make you uncomfortable.

It demands that you get comfortable in the discomfort. Get used to it. Otherwise, you'll be lulled into only doing what's comfortable. What's most comfortable is the familiar, and if it's familiar, then you've done it before. If you want to go *beyond* who you've been and what you've done, then you must be willing to embrace discomfort and know it's a natural part of the process. Comfort kills aliveness.

As I've shared, one of the big barriers in considering climbing Aconcagua was the fear of heights.

Fear is one of the biggest reasons you should explore your Big Thing. Just *thinking* about it will bring up the excuses and false beliefs that may be in the way. Those same fears and beliefs have been holding you back in other aspects of your life. Fears like: *I don't have what it takes. Who do I think I am anyway? I don't deserve it.* Fear is *not* a good reason to avoid your Big Thing. It is the exact reason why you *must*. Scary can be fun. You'd pay good money for a ride like this at Disneyland.

3. It may seem impossible
A good indicator that you're considering your Big Thing is that you have moments when you believe it's impossible. Yet you occasionally glimpse how it might succeed. Perhaps you believe the timing, funding, or circumstance makes the pursuit impossible. In some cases, what seems impossible is the reality of doing your Big Thing right *now*.

As I flip-flopped on the decision to climb Aconcagua, I couldn't see how it was possible. Yes, I knew it was theoretically possible—if I were older, stronger, and richer. Yet, based on my experience and my perception of what I was capable of, I didn't think I could actually do it then, and, to be honest, that was true. There were real challenges to overcome. It was a long shot, but that is what was so exciting— the idea that I might step beyond who I had been and become the person I wanted to be.

A common thought that often bubbles up for people when considering their Big Thing is, "Who am I to do this?" It certainly came up for me. I believed this expedition was selfish and frivolous. If I was still scraping by financially, I didn't deserve to spend this much money on myself and my dreams. Certainly, my family saw it that way. They knew how much debt I was in. Are you saying some version of this to yourself? If so, you may be dancing with your Big Thing.

DOUG LEIBINGER:
"POSSIBLE" IS A STATE OF MIND

Doug was a real estate broker on the brink of financial collapse. Like many during 2008 when the market was tanking, Doug was highly leveraged, with a big mortgage and three children. He feared losing it all.

I asked Doug what he wanted to create. He kept repeating his fears of losing everything. It was like pulling teeth at first because he was so focused on his circumstances. I challenged Doug to consider not only what would get him by, but also pushed him farther to identify what would make this the best year of his life.

He said he wanted to be one of the top ten brokers in Aspen, generating more than $50 million per year in sales, and flying on private jets to meet with clients to close deals. His deeper desires were about family; the trips they would take, the fun they would have, and the experiences that would expand his girls' education and growth.

Doug clarified what he wanted, but he was afraid of the plummeting real estate market, and he feared that going for this Big Thing at a time when he was so stressed was impossible—even irresponsible.

I helped Doug articulate who he would have to be, and then coached him into it. In less than two years, Doug became one of the top ten brokers in Aspen. He came out of nowhere to be a trendsetter at a time when most brokers were accepting defeat. He has since far surpassed the goals he laid out in our early conversations. In fact, his total sales in 2021 were $273 million, and he's currently in the #1 position. Perhaps most gratifying is the number of nonprofits and causes that Doug continues to contribute to through his success. He's also been able to create meaningful and enriching learning opportunities with his family that he says are priceless.

Doug wouldn't be where he is today had he not decided to step beyond his fear and limiting thoughts to say "yes" to his Big Thing, even though it seemed impossible during that economy. It's never a convenient time to transform your life. The only time that really matters is now.

A Big Thing wakes up the bigger part of you. The smaller part of you, the more fearful part, says the opposite. It says, "Be practical. You'll be disappointed. You'll get hurt. You'll look silly and ridiculous, and you'll fail." Because this was Doug's Big Thing, it inspired him in a way that simply "surviving the downturn" would not have given him. Your Big Thing may seem impossible, but it's seeking *you* as much as you're seeking it. Have the courage to follow your Big Thing regardless of the circumstances.

4. The how may (temporarily) elude you

Not knowing *how* is one of the biggest blocks that keep people from going for their Big Thing. Most people think they need to know how before deciding to take it on. Knowing how is not a prerequisite. You can figure it out along the way.

The how is often revealed in stages, like climbing a long, steep staircase. You see a step in front of you, but you can't yet see the landing. You step up onto that first step, and then the next, and the next until the landing becomes visible. Sometimes you see the next five or ten steps, but you must take each step in turn to get to the top.

If you're stuck, you may be hung up on the *how*. You haven't yet figured exactly how you're going to reach your Big Thing, so you don't commit. Perhaps you're obsessing on the *how* before getting crystal clear on the *what*. Don't worry about the how for now.

5. You need help to realize it

Because your Big Thing is big, you'll need assistance. You'll have to build a team and surround yourself with support. Often your team will include people who believe in you and want to see you do well. These may be friends and family, while others may be coaches or mentors. You may hire some of this support, and you may get creative in how you assemble your team.

This also builds a supportive network, and lets people clearly know what you stand for. It's empowering to be seen by others. It also fortifies you, as others will hold you accountable to this wonderful vision.

I'm not sure where I picked this up, but somewhere I started to believe that if I had to ask for help, I had no business doing it. I should be able to do it myself. Asking for support was a sign of weakness. It's cheating. If I got help, I might become dependent. Not only did I think it was weak to accept help, but also doubly uncool to ask. If I couldn't do it alone, I avoided it. This snowballed into major challenges. More than anything, it kept my life from getting bigger than myself.

It took getting into serious debt before I could admit needing help. This humiliated the part of me that believed help was for wimps, but it also opened me up to see that no one does anything meaningful by themselves. Understanding that it's important to receive help makes it possible to go for your Big Thing.

Does an athlete who's committed to Olympic gold think it's weak to have a coach? Does a CEO think it's weak to consult a Board of Directors? Then why on earth would you think it's weak to enlist support with your Big Thing?

Are you trying to go it alone? This attitude must change if you're to go for your Big Thing.

*"If you can do it on your own,
then it's not a Big Thing."*

6. You must transform in order to reach it

You can't realize your Big Thing by being the person you've been up 'til now. What got you here won't get you there. A Big Thing demands transformation and bringing out the bigger, brighter, and bolder parts of you that have been dormant. This is not saying there's something wrong with you now. This doesn't imply that who you are and how you've shown up has been weak. What I'm saying here is that no matter how successful you've been, there's more of your life that's trying to get out. There's more strength. There's more vitality. There's more ingenuity. It's not that you're lacking anything. It's that there's so much more trying to get out.

Your Big Thing has many layers. One of the greatest elements is its ability to change you for the better. This is the real reason your endeavor is so important. If you want to unlock even greater power from within, it will take something significant to coax it out. Simple goals will not summon this power from your inner depths. Only your Big Thing can do that.

If you could realize your Big Thing by being the person you are today, then it's not a Big Thing.

7. It will serve others

You may not see *how* your Big Thing will change the world, but if that's your intent, it will reveal itself in due time. Intending to serve through your Big Thing can elevate your Big Thing to make an even greater impact.

ROBIN:
WALKING OFF WALL STREET

Following his inner compass, Robin left a lucrative Wall Street career to pursue a heightened sense of purpose. He joined a nonprofit that was saving children's lives in Haiti.

He wasn't seeing how this could have an even bigger impact, which was his intention. In one of my seminars, he saw an even bigger vision for what he was doing. He shifted the mission from saving lives, to the idea that one of their orphanages would raise a future president of Haiti. This was both unreasonable and bold. It was not born out of something outside of Robin; it arose from within. He would later say God inspired it, but he's the first to tell you that if he hadn't slowed down and asked himself these questions, he never would have heard that voice.

Days after his realization, he met with his team, and they integrated this new vision into the organization. They committed to it as a team and began developing this vision. Within weeks, Robin met with Haitian politicians and dignitaries from nearby countries. He negotiated for them to provide full college scholarships for a number of students from their orphanages.

Your Big Thing will impact more than just you. Intending to serve through your Big Thing has the power to alter history. Robin would attest that he's merely one man who wants to make a difference, but if that vision and boldness gets bogged down in the narrow thinking of day-to-day concerns, we all lose.

While these seven signposts may seem like they're telling you to turn back, they're actually *confirmation* you're on the right path.

A Big Goal vs. A Big Thing

Maybe you're successful and achieving, and have accomplished big goals, but this doesn't necessarily mean you're going after your Big Thing. Very often, high achievers come to my office looking for a breakthrough they have yet to experience. Despite significant outer success, they feel and know there's more for them, another gear they yearn to experience to elevate their entire life.

A Big Thing is not simply an outcome to achieve. It's a mountaintop daring you to touch it. It's more than a goal because it holds special meaning for you. Your Big Thing will catalyze you in a way that a mere goal cannot.

STEVE MILLER:
BIG GOALS WILL NOT IGNITE YOU
LIKE YOUR BIG THING

I was facilitating a group of fifteen multi-unit restaurant owners on a one-day retreat to support them in uncovering their Big Thing. They were discussing who they'd have to be as individuals, and, as a team, to create their Big Thing. It was an incredible day, and the focus of the conversation was, "What's your Big Thing, inside your business?"

The leader of the group, Steve Miller, said, "My Big Thing is to lose 30 pounds."

I pressed back, because a Big Thing is more than a goal. It demands that you be someone new in order to realize it. "That sounds more like a big goal than a Big Thing," I said. "You can lose 30 pounds. You already know how to do that."

He confessed, "Yeah. I know how to, but I haven't done it."

I kept pressing. "I suspect that's a step *on the way* to your Big Thing, but, if you achieved that, what would you want to do?"

"No. That *is* my Big Thing. Losing 30 pounds would have me at my fighting weight. That's the weight I was when I was at my best in my business. If I do that, I know it will change the game."

What I didn't know was that Steve was hesitant to share his Big Thing in front of his colleagues. He felt it might inhibit them in clarifying theirs. I learned this when I followed up six months later. "How are you doing with your Big Thing, releasing those extra 30 pounds?"

In a somber voice he admitted he was struggling. "I was inspired the first few weeks, but after that I really couldn't motivate myself. I actually added a few pounds."

I was sorry to hear that, but not surprised. I've met with countless people who, for some reason, were not willing to declare their Big Thing, and settled on something smaller, more doable. The problem with this logic is that a small outcome will only summon a small amount of energy from within. I asked if he was open to some coaching. He agreed.

"If you lose 30 pounds, what does it allow you to do?"

"Well, number one," he said. "I'll feel happier. I'll have more energy, and the confidence of knowing that I can put my mind to something and do it. My confidence was shaken during the downturn, and I lost a lot of money. It was really hard. Accomplishing this would prove that I could do this again."

I went further, "If you prove you could do it again, then what?"

"Well, I'll be confident. I'd feel great."

"And if you felt confident and great, then what?"

"I'd have the best year of my professional life in the restaurant business."

"And, Steve, if you accomplished that, then what?"

He said, "I would write a book."

Now I could feel a current of powerful energy emanating from him. It was vibrant and unmistakable. This was starting to get juicy. "Tell me more."

"In our company, I challenge members to read a book a month. We all read it and have powerful discussions about it, but I've always felt like there's no book that really addresses the unique and specific needs of the restaurant business today. I've always wished someone would write that book, but no one has. What I would do is write that book and teach those I serve, and I would do this so I could continue to be a leader in this space."

I had him pause and notice how he felt in his body. "What's present for you?"

He said, "I feel like I'm buzzing. I feel great. I feel lighter."

"Congratulations," I said. "You uncovered your Big Thing."

For the previous six months, he had struggled. He was not finding his way because he was avoiding his Big Thing. Your Big Thing changes the game. It dwarfs the other challenges.

Three months later, Steve called and said, "I'm on fire. I've lost 15 pounds, and I have not even worried about working out. It's a non-issue. I'm doing what needs to be done, and I've written a first draft."

To anchor this learning, I asked him, "To what do you attribute this sudden burst of power?"

"Having my Big Thing on the table put everything else in perspective. It woke me up. Now the challenges seem small in comparison. Not only do I have a draft of the book, but I'm also on track for the best year of my career." This is a vivid example of The Big Thing Effect.

CHAPTER 2

Know You Are More Than You Think

WHAT IF I <u>AM</u> READY?

June 5, 2010 • Glenwood Springs, Colorado

A week after I declined to join the Aconcagua team, the phone rang. It was Stephen.

"Hey Jeff, I've been thinking about you."

Ughh! Why did he have to call?! I was just getting comfortable with backing out. Now I was triggered. Some part of me felt like he was pushing me to do something I had clearly said "no" to. Yet, there was still a conflict broiling inside. I wanted to do the expedition, but I simply couldn't see how. I was transfixed on all the obstacles. Yet, Stephen calling back felt like a renegade had breached the castle gates and heard my soul's cry for help. I tried to brush him off, but it felt so reassuring to hear his voice.

He continued, "I know your email said you weren't ready for this project, and you also stated you have many other things going on, and that the timing was bad. But what if this *is* right for you? What if you *are* that guy who does stuff like this, and what if this challenge could help bring out that part of you?"

Although I was scared, this was music to my ears. Mentors often show up in ways that can be uncomfortable at first. While this collision of desire and fear was challenging, it was also enlivening. I confided with Stephen about the conflict brewing inside. While I really wanted to join, I feared that it might be irresponsible and would ultimately ruin me financially. Also, I didn't want to jeopardize the meager financial progress I'd made over the past few years. He listened and understood. He didn't push. Yet he did leave me with a question: "What if you *are* ready?"

Unlock the Gamechanger in You

Gamechanger: noun.
An event, idea, procedure, or person that
effects a significant shift in the current manner of
doing or thinking about something.

Doing your Big Thing requires becoming a gamechanger. When most of us think about that word, we think of people who have done something life changing and world changing. People like Steve Jobs and the way he revolutionized the world of computers, phones, the music industry, animation, and more. Or people like Misty Copeland, the first Black prima ballerina at American Ballet Theatre, who broke the racial glass ceiling around skin color and body type in the elitist world of ballet. Or people like Greta Thunberg, who as a teenager single-handedly decided to take on global leaders to inspire radical action about the climate crisis.

These people are indeed gamechangers, and they're among a small percentile of the population who will do something genuinely life changing and world changing. Though some of us may see ourselves and our Big Thing as falling into in this category of gamechanger, many do not.

And that's OK, because you don't need to be a gamechanger in the external, conventional sense of the word, to do your Big Thing. But you do need to become an *internal* gamechanger, to make a "significant shift in the current manner of doing or thinking about something." And that something is *you*. I'm talking about changing the game inside your own mind—the way you see yourself and approach your life.

The Seven Keys to Doing Your Big Thing will unlock the ga-mechanger in you so that you can take on what is truly calling you, no matter how "big" your Big Thing is. No matter how life changing and world changing for others, it will be life changing for *you*. Either way, the process and approach to bringing it to fruition are exactly the same.

The famous ad that Steve Jobs launched in 1997 after his return to Apple, proclaimed, "Here's to the crazy ones …. Because the people who are crazy enough to think that they change the world, are the ones who do." He was absolutely right. And I'm here to tell you, the people who are crazy enough to think that they can change *themselves* are also the ones who do.

The Essential Self vs. The Conditioned Self

We each have two "selves." There is the "Essential Self" and the "Conditioned Self." The essential you doesn't need to change. The essential you is your spirit, your soul, your essence. This is the deep intrinsic you that's been there all along.

The Conditioned Self is created by your thinking, your self-image, your story. It's your ego. When you change your story, you change the way you show up in the world. This will change your experience and alter the scope of what's possible.

To be a gamechanger, the first change happens within. Hold on. Before you resist and say, "I don't need changing. I'm just fine as I am," hear me out.

Lindsay and I are blessed with two daughters, Emory and Brooklyn. Their essence has been evident since birth. Although they will mature and change as they grow, that spirit, that essence, is in there. We see it. All parents understand this universal truth.

I'm not saying you need to change that part of you. That essential part of you needs nothing, but it does want something. It wants to shine, and it instinctively wants to shed any habits or ways of being that conceal its radiance.

As you move through life, you start to take on thoughts, beliefs, and behaviors that combine to create the Conditioned Self. You start to become someone who is farther from your essential self and constrained by your thoughts about the world around you. It's this Conditioned Self that we're working to change. We're choosing to transform the parts of the Conditioned Self that stand in the way of who you *truly* are, who you most want to be, and what you most want to contribute.

Shifting this Conditioned Self will allow more of your Essential Self to illuminate your humanity and touch the world through your hands. The exciting news is that you can begin making meaningful shifts in the Conditioned Self immediately. You don't have to wait for what you think you need in order to be the person you desire to be. Altering this conditioning will liberate your Essential Self.

The Power is Within You

You are so much more than you think. You're more than your education, intellect, or experience. You are spirit first, human second. More than superhuman, you are a super *being*.

I believe we are *spiritual* beings living a *human* experience. Said another way, I believe that we are, at our core, spiritually whole and complete, fully connected to infinite wisdom and power. Like a lamp is connected to the electric grid through the power outlet, you're connected to the power that creates all of life. This is your highest and deepest identity. We're also human.

"Humanity is the lampshade through which the spirit shines."

You are more than your immediate skill and function. You're even more than the miraculous interplay of matter and energy. There's a greater life seeking to live and express through you. You simply have to be aware of it and get out of the way. Rather than obsessing over your little fears and worries, realize that something much bigger is trying to happen through you. You are here for something special, and you're capable of so much more than you let yourself believe. Own the larger capacity that lives in you and know that you're capable of this greatness. We all have that power and possibility. It's what we were made for.

You're connected to the intelligence that has created all things; that power courses through your soul. Your soul is leading you, whether you're aware of it or not. But if you are unaware, you might mistakenly walk around thinking you're merely human. What we identify with determines our experience. If you identify with your spirit, and the infinite nature and qualities you can access through that spirit, you will feel empowered and strong.

"If you only identify with your body and your circumstances, with your conditioned self, you'll feel at the mercy of your mortality. Remembering your essential nature wakes you up to what's truly possible."

PREACHING TO THE CORN: EXPERIENCING MY TRUE SELF

I was two years old when my parents divorced in 1974. We lived on a farm three miles north of Worms, Nebraska, and I only got to see Dad one weekend a month. I lived for those weekends. The only one he missed was when a blizzard closed the Interstate. I was crushed.

Mom didn't have it easy as a single mother. She worked two jobs and did everything she could to care for me. I wanted nothing more than to be close to her, in the eye of her affection, but I didn't experience that affection very often because she struggled with intimacy and closeness. I would later come to learn she was reeling from her own journey of pain in the wake of traumatic experiences from her childhood.

As Mom self-medicated with alcohol, I looked for attention

anywhere I could find it, mostly from my maternal grandparents. But nothing matched the love I felt when I spoke with Dad on the phone each Wednesday at 7:00 p.m. We were limited to twenty minutes because the long-distance rates were expensive. I left each call feeling like things were going to be OK.

I remember one particular call when I was six. I was so happy to hear Dad's distinct and comforting voice. I felt I could do anything with his encouragement, but he was 100 miles away in the "big city" (population 6,000). I was full of emotion and struggled for words. He said that he wished things were different. He wished that we didn't have to go through this.

I twisted the curly cord around my fingers while recapping the events of the day. As the final two minutes approached, all I could do was cry. It must have broken my father's heart to have to patch me up for another week. Toward the end of our call he got serious and said, "Jeffrey, if I could take this from you I would, but I can't. This is the way it is right now. We're going to be OK." And then he said something I'll never forget.

"Jeffrey," he said. "As hard as this may be, there is a reason behind this. This will not hurt you. Instead, this will strengthen you. This is tempering on your steel."

I wiped away tears, trying not to breathe into the receiver. I wanted to be strong for Dad. We exchanged "I love you's," and I went back to the world from which I so badly wished to be rescued.

One weekend, in June 1978, Dad and his new girlfriend were bringing me back to the farm. Those car rides were fun, but the last 30 minutes were hell. It stung to realize that I was going back and would not have Dad's attention for another month.

This night, the smell of afternoon rain on fresh-cut alfalfa lingered in the air, causing Dad's hay fever to act up. Time for me to go back to the world of, "children are to be seen and not heard." I started to cry.

As I went to the trunk to get my bag, he was already walking up the steps to the front door. I could hear him apologizing for being late. Then he asked my mom, "Why can't I see Jeff more often? It's not fair we only get to see each other once a month." As I stepped up onto the porch, I saw Mom's livid face. Expletives flew.

My stepfather, Dale, pulled me into the house and slammed the door while Dad pleaded with them both to listen. Both Mom and Dale were yelling, and they ordered me to go to my room. Angry words filled the house, but they paled in comparison to the storm raging inside me. I had so much sadness, anger, and confusion boiling and no say in the matter.

I lay in the dark, drowning in these intense emotions. Why did my parents have to be divorced? Why couldn't I spend more time with my Dad? Why wouldn't anyone listen? I buried my head in the pillow and cried loud and hard. I hoped no one would hear. Surely, no one cared.

Minutes later, Dale entered the bedroom and sat on the edge of the bed. He tried his best to console me, but nothing could penetrate the rage and hurt. They were too strong. Because of their refusal to let me see Dad more frequently, and because of Mom's emotional distance, I felt all alone. When I looked at them, all I could think about was that they wanted to keep me from the one person who made me happy.

This emotional roller coaster was the monthly routine. I would return home after a weekend with Dad, then feel the punch-in-the-gut reality of living in a home where I felt invisible.

But thanks to Dad, I decided that there was a gift in the challenge, that it was actually making me stronger. That's what he meant by "tempering on my steel."

Life on the farm was simple, filled with outdoor chores, and nature, which I loved. I attended a small Lutheran school that served fifty-two kids—kindergarten through 8th grade—much like Little House on the Prairie. My mother, grandmother, and great-grandmother had all graduated from this three-room schoolhouse. The community was staunchly religious. There were seven kids in my class, including two pairs of twins. I was often in trouble because I challenged the religious lessons being taught. I couldn't buy into the idea that "God is love," yet non-believers were all going to Hell. I backed my arguments with Scripture, and locked horns in heated debates with teachers. Needless to say, they didn't appreciate the fiery backtalk. Most of my recesses were spent writing on the blackboard, "I will not disrespect my teachers."

One particular day, in fourth grade, the principal stood up in front of the entire school and admonished me. "Jeff Patterson, you are displaying a bad Christian attitude. Do you think God likes what you're doing? Do you think Jesus approves?"

I walked slowly to the front of the class, and, like a lawyer, demanded that he give me the written definition of a "Christian attitude" so I could follow its example. Then I continued. "Do you think God approves of *you* making fun of me? Do you think you're demonstrating love as Christ would?"

The kids just sat there wide-eyed, astonished that anyone would speak up to a teacher, much less the principal. I became the "troubled kid" and built an identity around it. I knew I would get into trouble and didn't even care.

I desperately wanted to be noticed, to be appreciated, to be special, but I kept hearing that I was a problem and that God didn't approve. By the time I was ten, I would wander the sandy pastures and cornfields for miles, crying and asking God why I was living such a painful life.

Why doesn't anybody like me? What's wrong with me? What did I do to deserve this? I kept praying, *God, do something good with my life. There's got to be more. Make me good. Help me!*

Then a miracle happened.

I paused in the waist-high rows of corn. The breeze rolled across the green fields until it brushed my face, loaded with the smell of honeysuckle and plum blossoms. I felt a warm presence pour into my head and slowly fill me up.

I began to feel peace, an otherworldly serenity. I stared up at the blue sky and felt as if it were a part of me. Everything went still, and, in that moment, I felt a calm that was so grounded and real, I couldn't remember being upset about anything. I didn't know who, or even where, I was. I simply *was*. Pure being. It was as if I were merged with the cornfields and the sky and the squeaking windmill. I felt one with everything, and I instantly knew everything was OK. It was *more* than OK. It was *great*.

My tears of sadness transformed into tears of gratitude. I looked west, mesmerized by the blazing sunset melting into pastels of pink and powder blue. My senses were alive, yet totally calm. I saw the horizon of my future, and it was bright and full of joy.

I basked in this feeling for a few minutes, until I couldn't contain the intensity of it any longer. It was as if someone were telling me I was made for something special in this life, and this exact experience was honing me, tempering me for it. A volcano of passion, purpose, and positivity erupted out of me. I started preaching, as if I had a congregation, and the message was, "You can do it! You can do anything! Anything is possible!" I was preaching to the fence posts, to the cattle, to the corn. "You can do it, you can grow! You'll be knee-high by the 4th of July!"

I continued to walk and speak as this powerful feeling guided my words, and I was moved to tears as I spoke. I could feel my spirit. I could feel God's hand and sense my future.

This became a regular thing. I would come home from school, and, after chores, would go out into the fields and walk and pray and cry for miles, until that calm, blissful feeling washed over me again. It gave me hope and joy and inspiration. When I felt this way, I would erupt with motivational verse. There was energy behind it. It was not to be kept inside.

One spring day while delivering this message, I felt as if something or someone was following me. I turned around and saw a host of translucent people, thousands of them, walking behind me. They covered the pasture, standing in silence, waiting for me to speak. I didn't know exactly what this meant, but I had a distinct inner knowing that this was a glimpse into my future.

For many years, I tried to determine what to do with this

experience. While I may not have known what my future would look like at the time, I was beginning to get a taste of who I was meant to be, who I really *was*. I felt that I was meant to help others know that their dreams were possible. There was this inner sense and knowing that my future was about using my voice to inspire, uplift, and help people walk ahead in life. I began to welcome the pain and challenge of life because it would draw me into this destiny.

Reconnecting to Your Essential Self

Have you ever experienced a moment when you felt the power of life coursing through you? When you felt one with everything, and understood, deep in your heart, that you not only had a place in this world, but a special place, one that only you could fulfill? Remember that moment and recall the deep and powerful experience.

As you recall this memory it will trigger the same powerful feelings, and they will begin to radiate through you. It will bring back the part of you that experienced it. This is the Essential Self, and it's as real as the nose on your face. Many of us identify with our human attributes so intently that we forget the magic that lives within and through us. This is what kept me stuck, and it's what had me say "no" to Stephen's invitation. I was identifying with my situation and limitation. I had forgotten the true magic, the deeper part that was pulsing just below the fear and limited thinking.

We Become Our Identity

Your life will reflect that with which you most identify. Which aspect of your life do you identify with the most? Your job? Your accomplishments? Your failures? We all have a tendency to identify strongly with some part of our life. The question is, which part? Some people identify with their education. They take enormous pride in their intellect and the advanced degrees they've worked hard to earn. Others identify with their achievements, amassing shelves of trophies of one sort or another.

There are some who identify with their mistakes, either one big error—like a failed marriage or quitting college—or the string of mistakes they perceive they've been cursed to live out. You can bet that within moments of meeting them, they'll either reference it, or this identification will color their communication. Some people are deeply identified with others' opinions of them. They're consumed with winning approval and being liked. This takes enormous energy and usually ends in frustration.

You can see the importance of getting honest with yourself about what you're identifying with most. What you identify with will radiate brightly in your being. It will magnify through your thoughts, feelings, and behaviors. In its simplest form, you identify most with that which you give the most attention.

If you're to realize your true potential, start by loosening your over-identification with your intellect, education, skills, experience, family name, etc. Loosen your identification with transient thoughts and emotions. Instead, identify with your magic, your Essential Self. Believe it or not, we've all had at least one experience of our Essential Self. Maybe yours didn't occur in the waist-high cornfields of Nebraska, but you've had your own, even if you've forgotten or overlooked it.

Reminding yourself of this deeper nature opens you to the possibility that you are here for greatness. Recalling your Essential Self will give you an experience that mere understanding cannot.

GEORGE:
RECALLING AN EXPERIENCE
OF HIS ESSENTIAL SELF

I asked my client George to do this. He described a moment more than a decade ago, on the side of a road in Tuscany, where he lay bleeding after crashing his bicycle. As he recalled the sensation of life draining away, he could also feel a strength and vibrancy inside that he had never felt so fully before. Despite being in intense pain, he also felt a quality of peace and joy that was even greater. "I felt an amazing connection with everything, and I had no worry or fear," he told me, "even as I was being airlifted to the nearest hospital."

As George continued to recount this near-death experience, he was reinvigorated. I could see it in his eyes; they were radiant. When we wrapped up our conversation, he said he felt incredible, and it makes sense when you think about it. Because George, just like you and me, is always walking around with this incredibly huge and wonderful spirit, but we forget it's there. Sometimes it takes an abrupt situation to slow down our mind and body to actually experience it. As George recounted the events and let himself re-experience that moment, he re-connected with his Essential Self.

Remember Who You Are

Yes, let's acknowledge our intellect and celebrate our accomplishments. Let's appreciate our heartaches, but let's not identify them as "who we are." When you move through life knowing there's a part of you that is *so* big it cannot be destroyed, there is a confidence, a certainty in your step. By actually experiencing the energy of greatness inside, you can directly sense that something great is possible. If the thing you want to do *seems* impossible, you will need this added power. When your old habits and identities attempt to stop you from moving forward, this experience will drive you beyond limitations into a new realm of possibility.

Doing this will have you begin to realize that there's nothing missing in you. There is no lack or limitation. You are whole and complete. You're more than enough. In fact, the things that you don't have make up your unique presence in this world. If you own that, if you appreciate and relish that uniqueness, your spirit can shine through and elevate your life to a whole new level of artistry.

Exercise:
Remembering Your Essential Self

Now it's your turn. Like George, recall a moment from your past where you felt the presence of your Essential Self, a magical moment where you felt one with everything, and that it's all going to be OK. Trust what memory comes up for you.

Close your eyes and take yourself back to that memory. Imagine the moment coming to life before your very eyes and see yourself firmly planted in that situation. Let it come alive in your mind and let your senses awaken. Notice any sounds, smells, or sensations. Now, re-experience that moment, and most importantly, that feeling.

After re-experiencing this peak moment, you can let go of the memory and hold onto the feeling. You are not simply feeling the memory; you are feeling your spirit.

When you *experience* this feeling of your Essential Self, you'll sense that you're capable of greatness. It's not a mental thing—it's a sensation you cannot deny. Cultivating this sensation from within is at the heart of many great spiritual traditions. When you *experience* this energy inside of you, it lessens your need for a belief about it. I call this deeper experience, *knowing*. When you *know* something, it goes beyond mental belief.

CHAPTER 3

Clarify Your Vision

MY VISION CLEARED UP
MY CONFUSION

June 20, 2010 • Glenwood Springs, Colorado

I bolted upright, wide awake again, and *again* it was 3:00 a.m. This time of night had become my witching hour, haunting me about this decision. A week ago, I'd nervously sent the email to Stephen saying "no," but I couldn't stop thinking about the possibility. I was still conflicted. The indecision was driving me crazy.

As I lay awake, the question Stephen had left me with rolled over and over in my mind— "What if you *are* ready?" I started to imagine that I was, and what successfully climbing Mt. Aconcagua would mean. I began to envision myself standing on the summit, and how good that would feel. I imagined the camaraderie and helping my teammates along the way. I even considered how my growth and lessons might positively impact the clients and companies I served. Suddenly, what started as a crazy idea was now beginning to enlarge and take on specific shape. I grabbed my journal and started writing feverishly.

I scribbled everything I hoped would occur on this expedition, including what I wanted it to lead to. I was not saying "yes" yet, but I was exploring what I wanted to have unfold if I did. I wrote about how I wanted to speak to audiences about my lessons on the mountain and how this might lead to writing books. I wrote about how my climbing experience would benefit my coaching clients because they would see me pushing the boundaries of my own fears and limitations.

I was on fire with inspiration as I continued writing. I noticed that this vision was not something new. These possibilities had been ruminating for years. I had long dreamed of climbing mountains and tying these experiences into my coaching work. Suddenly, I became grateful that this decision was so challenging because it forced me to look deeper and explore what I *really* wanted.

There were a million reasons to say "no" to this expedition. It was important that I start looking for the reasons to say "yes."

Writing all of this down helped to tease apart the confusion. When I saw it spelled out on the page, I began to feel as if I were already on the expedition. I was hot with excitement. Previously it was an overwhelming idea, but now it was a clear picture of what I wanted this adventure to lead to, and I could see it with color and specificity.

The Power of Visualizing Your Future

Have you ever seen something in your future before it actually happened? Maybe you wanted something so badly that you started imagining it as if it were materializing right in front of you. Perhaps you closed your eyes and let yourself be swept away by the images, sounds, and sensations of your desire. In my experience, some things can be imagined easily, while others can be difficult to visualize. Sometimes, a challenge can help inspire the full clarity of your Big Thing.

A few years ago, I was traveling in Rwanda with Robert, a dear friend and client. His Big Thing is helping people in need get a leg up. He was invested in several businesses in Rwanda, and we were there to see the impact of his work, and also advise the organizations where we could. In preparation for our trip, he urged me to read several books. One book was *Left to Tell* by Immaculée Ilibagiza. Immaculée brings to life the brutal events of her youth during the horrific 1994 genocide in Rwanda. She was hunted by the warring Hutus for months and found refuge in a tiny hidden bathroom in a small home. Most of her Tutsi family had been murdered. The Hutu were attempting to wipe out the entire Tutsi tribe on the basis that they were inferior human beings. We visited her village and saw the very location where this horror unfolded.

To survive, Immaculée lay silent, crammed inside the wall of her neighbor's bathroom. She feared for her life while her siblings were being brutally murdered outside the house. If she were discovered, she would meet the same fate. While crouched for months in this cramped space, she would imagine speaking English (something she could not do at the time). She also envisioned teaching people in English and sharing her story in places like the United Nations. She visualized it every day, as if it were real. What's so moving about this woman's story is that she's now a well-known author who tours the world speaking about equality and peace. The visions she imagined in that bathroom are now her life. She had every reason to be scared and focus on all of the bad that could happen. Instead, she focused on a future that inspired her, despite the horrid conditions of the moment.

While your Big Thing may not be this intense, the principle of seeing your future is every bit as important. Just clarifying your Big Thing can transform your life.

HAYSEED GOES TO HOLLYWOOD: VISIONING MY FUTURE INTO REALITY

When I was ten, my dad and stepmother took me to Los Angeles on a family vacation. Being a Nebraska farm boy, the thought of city lights and movie stars fascinated me.

We did many of the typical tourist activities, but the highlight was our day at Universal Studios Hollywood. I was ecstatic with delight. I'd never seen so much color and excitement. The backlot tour and the shows were so inspiring. I even got to sit in "Kit," the famous "Night Rider" car.

One of my requests was to see a particular live stage show

that was playing in a theater on the lot because they brought up kids from the audience to participate. I wanted my chance! We climbed the steps into the theater and waited for the show to start. A Snickers bar and the world's largest soda had me out of my mind on sugar.

Music thumped. A confetti cannon blasted above the crowd as the host ran on to the stage. He opened with a few jokes, then announced that he was looking for *one* lucky kid to come up to help host this show! I shot three feet off of the bench, waving both hands in the air, yelling, "Me, me, me!" Every kid in the theater called out, "Me, me, me!"

The host scanned the audience looking for the perfect candidate. I looked like a rabbit directing traffic, arms flailing, jumping with excitement.

My voice was getting hoarse, and I was growing frustrated. Surely, he saw me. He looked near me, over me, around me, but he never *saw* me. I stared at Dad in disbelief. Then the host pointed to a little girl in the third row and she ran up onto the stage. I was crushed.

Choking back tears, I dropped my head. Dad saw my disappointment and put his arm around my shoulder. "Jeffrey, someday *you* are going to host *that* show on *that* stage."

I thought, "Yeah right!" I lived on a farm in the middle of nowhere. I was the class buffoon. *Nobody* liked me, not even my teachers. I could *never* be on stage like *that* guy. That's what I thought, but what I said was, "Do you really think so?"

"I don't think so," Dad said. "I *know* so."

That exchange was a turning point. He planted the seed of a Big Thing. For the rest of that show, I imagined how I would hold the microphone. I visualized the kids I'd pick from the audience. I was inspired and starting to believe Dad's words.

Three days later Dad dropped me back at the farm, and I went back to feeding cattle, shoveling manure, and being ridiculed at school. When times got tough, I'd imagine being on that stage. That dream helped me through an emotionally turbulent childhood. That dream became my Big Thing.

As time went on, the dream faded. I graduated from high school and eventually studied journalism at University of Nebraska. In broadcasting class, I got comfortable in front of the camera and landed a job hosting a popular sports show on ESPN2. I'd found what I loved to do, but it wasn't easy. Hosting jobs came and went, but I stayed committed and picked up other work along the way, once even singing in a theme park.

In March of 1996, I got a call from a producer for Nickelodeon. He had seen my work on the sports show and asked if I'd like to work with him on a new project.

"We are producing our first-ever live game show at Universal Studios Hollywood. We want you to move to Los Angeles and host it."

So, I loaded my '89 Honda Accord with everything I owned and drove to L.A. It was a huge step. As rehearsals began, my excitement was immediately tempered by the intense schedule to learn so much material so quickly. Several executives were critiquing from every angle. The director was extremely tough, demanding, impatient, and loud. He would cut me off in the middle of a line, and scream, "That SUCKS! Do it AGAIN!" The pressure was overwhelming.

On the eve of my 25th birthday, I called Dad. We were two weeks away from opening.

"Dad, I'm not cut out for this. Who am I kidding? I'm just a farm boy from Nebraska."

After a long pause, he said, "Jeffrey, do you remember when you were little and we went to Universal Studios?"

"Yes."

"And do you remember, when the host didn't pick you, how upset you were?"

"Yes."

"And do you remember what I said?"

The whole scene came flooding back—the noise, the excitement, the disappointment.

With tears welling, I whispered, "You said that someday I was going to host *that* show on *that* stage."

Dad cleared his throat, "And look at where you are right now."

I was stunned. I had completely forgotten.

The next morning, I shared this story with the crew. One of the producers, Chris Durmick, jumped up saying, "I remember that show; it was actually held right here, where this theater now stands, and I was the host."

That Big Thing, the dream of someday "hosting *that* show on *that* stage," pulled me through some of the darkest moments of my childhood. It helped me to see more than challenges. It gave me hope. More importantly, it gave me a focus that changed me. And the amazing thing is that I had eventually forgotten it, but it hadn't forgotten me. Those early days of visualizing my Big Thing somehow had literally led me to *that* show on *that* stage.

Just identifying your Big Thing will change you and your future. Visualizing it will accelerate it. Like a seed being watered, each time you visit the vision of your Big Thing, its roots grow deep.

When the Vision is Clear the Resources Appear

Many people rush into an idea and, before they clarify the vision, they start obsessing about *how*. Don't get me wrong; there must be strategy and action. You must clarify how you will reach your goal, but not before you clarify the outcome.

The means appear when the result is clear. It's essential to clarify your Big Thing before you map out a strategy. As with all meaningful strategies, the first part of the plan must include getting absolutely clear on what the target is.

Take a moment to reflect on this question: "If I had a Big Thing, what would it be?" If the answer is, "I don't know," then guess. What comes up for you? Clarify the what, and suspend the how for now. Once you catch a hint of your Big Thing, it's essential to write it down. It will change and grow and shift. Start with what is clear and don't fret what isn't.

Clarify the end goal by getting as specific as you can. In the beginning there can be some things that are not totally clear. That's OK. But own it, and stand in what *is* clear. The rest will emerge in perfect time.

Exercise:
Future Vision
(Part 1: Visualization)

I lead many clients through a process I call "Future Vision" where they imagine what they desire coming to pass. They begin to see it and feel it, so much so they can taste it. We're going to do this exercise together.

Before we start, it's important to know that there's no right (or wrong) way to do this exercise. It's creative and is not meant to be over-analyzed. Just have fun with it and trust what comes forward for you. Most of all, notice what you see, smell, feel or touch. Let your senses come alive, and trust what you experience. You might hear sounds, voices, or music. You may see colors and get a "sense" of something. You may also "feel" what it is. You can then begin to fill in the vision and eventually write it down.

Also, before we begin, consciously give yourself permission to see, hear, feel, and experience your Big Thing. In this visualization, you may actually see it, hear it, or sense it. Trust whatever shows up in whatever form it arrives. Keep in mind, you're not committing to anything here. Don't worry about what does, or does not, show up, how you'll get there, or if it's even possible.

This process involves deep listening to what is already trying to emerge. It also requires your imagination to fill in the gaps. As you do this, feel free to edit, alter and refine the vision. You're never locked in. This is a fun exercise, and, when done consistently, yields surprising results.

Guided
Visualization:

Imagine standing at the foot of a majestic mountain. Just ahead is a trail that leads through a grove of pines, and zigzags up the steep slope. Before you start walking, set an intention to experience clarity regarding your Big Thing. When you're ready, start walking. Feel the dirt and pebbles beneath your boots, notice that your footing and balance are steady. You're energized and ready to hike to the summit.

As you walk uphill through the forest, let your senses come alive. Feel the warm sunshine and smell the pines around you. You're enjoying this hike because you know that at the top you are going to come face-to-face with your Big Thing. This excites you. Notice everything you can about your surroundings: the trees, the temperature, the sky. As you continue up the trail, you emerge from the forest, and you can see the mighty peak staring down from its clouded perch. The grade is now steeper, your eyes steady on the trail while you switchback up the mountain. Your legs are strong and your lungs are clear.

Allow yourself to notice all your surroundings. Observe how blue and clear the sky is, the colors of the rock, and shrubs of oak and cedar as you pass. You're climbing higher and higher, getting closer to the summit. Notice the view, how small the trees below now look. A hawk glides by on the breeze, watching you ascend. Notice its brown wings and patches of red and white, its piercing wild call as it glides ahead.

You're close now. You can see the summit. You make the last few turns and make your way to the top. You stand tall and safely on the summit. See your hiking boots and the mountain beneath. You've made it. As you gaze upward, you notice a large rectangular rock. It looks like a bench, the perfect place to stand and take in the view.

You stand on the rock and turn 360 degrees surveying the expansive sky. Notice the puffy clouds below, and look back down the trail that brought you here. You've come a long way.

Sit on the rock bench for a moment and rest. To your left, you notice the trail continues down the other side of the mountain, disappearing in a bank of clouds. In a moment, someone very special is going to come up this trail to meet you. This special someone has important information to give you about your Big Thing. This visitor is you, from two years in the future.

Take a moment to open your heart and mind. Look down into the clouds as this figure emerges. As your Future Self approaches, trust what you see and sense. Look into their eyes. Notice the smile. Welcome your Future Self; invite them to sit next to you. Notice every detail about your Future Self. What are they wearing? What do you notice most? What stands out? What's different about this version of yourself? What quality of being are they most exuding? What adjective would you use to best describe them?

Your Future Self takes a seat right next to you. In a moment, they're going to give you a very important insight about your Big Thing. Open your mind and heart and allow yourself to receive the message they have traveled so far to share. Be open to the way your Future Self communicates with you. They might speak, you might see images, or you might feel what they are communicating. No matter how they communicate, trust what you receive.

Now, there may be a question you want to ask your Future Self. Let it be the most important question on your mind relating to your Big Thing. Ask, and once again, allow yourself to receive the response.

Simply be present, enjoying the conversation, receiving whatever comes up. What do you see, hear, or sense as you take in this guidance from your Future Self? You might have another follow-up question or two. Take as much time as you need to pose these questions, allowing yourself to receive the answers and feedback that directly relate to your Big Thing.

Now, after asking your questions and receiving the responses, your Future Self pulls out an iPad. They turn on the device and you instinctively know you're about to see images and videos of you and your Big Thing, and you're eager to view them. Have fun and trust what you see, hear, and sense. Notice everything you can about these images. The time, the place, the expression on your face. What do you know to be true as you watch it unfold? Observe what you're wearing and the qualities of being you are emitting. Be aware of any other people, locations, or images.

Intently observe and trust what comes up. Your Future Self scrolls to a screen that is a video of you in your Big Thing. Touch the red play icon with your finger and watch the video. There may be multiple videos that play... enjoy as you watch yourself fully living in the vibrancy and success of your Big Thing.

After you've asked your questions and viewed the images, take a moment to *thank* your Future Self for their presence, this special conversation, and for the insight. Acknowledge them with a handshake, a hug, or a high five. Take them in. This is *you*, two years from now. Feel assured that they are always available to speak with you whenever you wish. You thank them, and your Future Self makes their way back to the trail and begins their descent into the clouds.

Take a moment to let it all sink in. Feel the flat rock bench beneath you, the breeze on your neck, and the insight you've received from this visitor. Trust the experience and know it will, in some way, inform your Big Thing, even if you don't see how it will all fit together.

When you're ready, stand up and stretch your legs. Take in the view again before you leave. See the path back down the mountain. Take a deep breath, locking in the insight and clarity shared by your Future Self. Begin your steady descent back down the mountain. As you descend you notice footprints from your earlier ascent. What a journey it's been. You reflect on the experience and the insight you gained. Most of all, you feel the vitality of coming face-to-face with your Future Self. You swiftly move down along the trail. The hawk circles so close you can almost touch it. His high-pitched call shakes you even more awake. What an incredible experience! You move downhill through the forest. It seems smaller somehow, and even more pungent. Your senses are alive and everything seems brighter, clearer, more vibrant. You see the trailhead and reach it. You turn one last time to look back at the summit high above. Amazing to think you were there, and are now back, and all that you experienced in between. Take in one last deep breath and hold it, locking in the insight, the clarity and the experience. Then let it all go.

If, during the exercise, you didn't see or experience a lot of clarity, don't be alarmed. A client recently confided that, after doing this visualization in one of our early sessions, he struggled with the exercise. He said he couldn't see anything and was being hard on himself for not "getting it right." I assured him that it was working, even if it seemed empty of insight. I encouraged him to trust whatever came up (or didn't) and also the timing. If you didn't see anything, or this was a struggle for you, please know it's nothing to worry about.

Less than a week later, this client shared that he started being inspired by ideas and images that were popping into his head throughout his day. These were mental pictures, visions of him doing his Big Thing. In a conversation, while driving and even while working out, he began thinking about his Big Thing, and it started to take shape. Because of this, remember to be accepting of whatever comes up for you during and after this exercise. Keep your eyes, ears, and mind open. Regardless of your experience with this exercise, know that it can continue to inspire you long after you do it.

When It's Written It's Real

One great way to create clarity on your Big Thing is to write down what you want to have occur. Simply write down everything you can possibly think of that's clear about it on paper (or type if that works better for you). I find that putting literal pen to paper activates something tactile and visceral that primes the pump and gets things moving.

It never fails to amaze me how simple, yet effective, this

process is. Something profound happens when you take the elements, no matter how faint, and write them out. They become more than ideas. They become physical things—words on a page. Those words are touchstones to the soul of your Big Thing, and you will now be able to start working with them.

Exercise:
Future Vision
(Part 2: Writing)

Now that you've gone through the conversation with your Future Self, it's time to write down everything you possibly can about the experience. Putting this on paper will light up your creative brain. The writing often brings forward even more awareness.

Write down any clues or insights you've had about your Big Thing. How did this visualization inform you about your Big Thing? Perhaps your Future Self confirmed what you already know. Or maybe they shared something completely new. Write down any insight, detail, or feeling that might be related to your Big Thing. Capture as many details as possible to deepen your clarity. Here are some questions that might spark your writing:

- What stood out about your Future Self?
- What quality of being best describes your Future Self? (i.e., Present, Inspired, Disciplined, Collaborative, etc.)
- What message did you receive from your Future Self?
- What advice did they give you?
- Can you describe some of the images that popped up on the iPad?
- Were there any people you recognized?
- Did you notice any specific locations where you were engaging in your Big Thing?
- What was obvious about you in these images of you doing your Big Thing?

- What *quality of being* oozed from you in these images and videos?
- What was *different* about you in these videos compared to you now?
- What occurred that you want to remember?
- What is clearer now than before?
- What else do you want to remember from this experience?
- What is clearer now about your Big Thing?

Focus on What *is* Clear

You can only focus on one thing at a time, and what you focus on expands. Are you concentrating on what you desire, or obsessing on what you fear? Are you consistently looking at the picture of your Big Thing, or are you fixated on your doubts? If you focus intently on the vision of your Big Thing, you contribute to it expanding.

Have you ever noticed that when you focus on something, it begins to grow? Here's a little science to back this up. There's a part of your brain called the Reticular Activation System (RAS). Its job is to gather images and data that *match* what you focus on. If you're fixated on all the bad stuff, then your RAS is going to start looking for more of those patterns. That's why it's important to use the RAS consciously. It grows in response to your mind's clarity and the excitement of its fulfillment expands in your emotions. The RAS actually starts working to bring to you inputs that match those images.

This explains the phenomenon of Selective Perception. When you buy a new car, you suddenly see that car on the road everywhere. This is your RAS on high alert.

The same works when you focus on what you fear. If you focus on not having your Big Thing, you start to see all the obstacles. It seems like there's actually more evidence opposing what you desire, but that perception is the product of your focus. You can change this immediately by redirecting attention back onto your Big Thing.

As you engage in the process of clarifying your Big Thing, it's important to focus on what *is* clear, no matter how small. Bring your attention to what's clear rather than obsessing on what isn't.

Don't Compare

Your Big Thing is inspiring to *you* and should not be compared to anyone else's pursuits. Have the courage to listen to the unique desires inside of what you most want to create in your life. Listen to the small voice within that's leading you and don't discount your Big Thing for any reason. If you compare it to others, it may have you doubt what's emerging, and keep you from actually seeing it.

JOEL:
COMPARING IS CRIPPLING

In February of 2019, I led a group of sixteen executives in a Gamechanger Retreat in Beverly Hills. Joel, a thirty-five-year-old business owner and CEO, was frustrated and visibly distraught.

"Everybody here knows their Big Thing, but I don't have a clue."

"Are you open to some coaching?" I asked.

"Yes."

"I invite you to feel the rich emotion that's coming up for you."

He winced. "I feel tremendous sadness."

"Where?"

"In my stomach."

"So, let your attention go to your stomach and just feel the sensations."

His energy began to soften and calm.

"I don't know if this has anything to do with anything, but I've always dreamed of traveling America in an RV for a year with my family. I haven't thought about that for a long time."

Joel thought this idea seemed less altruistic than some of

the Big Things the other participants had shared, saying, "But this isn't a big idea. It's not helping the homeless, or saving the environment."

After further exploration, Joel realized that this RV pilgrimage was, in fact, his Big Thing. He mapped it against the seven tell-tale signs:

He deeply wanted it.

The thought of doing it scared him.

He thought it was impossible given the current circumstances.

He had no idea how to make it work.

He would need a lot of help from others.

He knew he would have to transform to realize this dream.

Finally, he wanted the *adventure* to inspire his family, and hopefully, others.

Boom! Textbook Big Thing!

Because he was *comparing* his endeavor to the Big Things of the other participants, his Big Thing was not visible to him. At first, the RV adventure seemed like an afterthought, and he discounted it. He had also buried this endeavor under the resigned belief that his time to pursue it had passed. As it turns out, he knew it all along but had been denying and suppressing it. Over the course of the retreat, his Big Thing finally wiggled its way to the surface.

Don't compare the dream that's emerging in you to anyone else's. This is also why it's important to be tenacious (and patient) when clarifying your Big Thing. It requires grit. The group applauded Joel's courage to speak up. The result was a huge breakthrough that everyone could feel. Deciding to go for it, he set a date and began planning.

Two years later, he returned, saying, "This adventure changed both me and my family in profound ways. In addition, our company grew significantly, despite my being away from the day-to-day."

Joel, and his family's experience, is also inspiring many

others who want to replicate their journey. He is now in post-production of a feature film that chronicles their adventure.

Let Yourself Want What You Truly Want

It can be tempting to get a little clarity and stop there. However, clarifying your Big Thing takes some persistence. It also helps to dig deeper and nudge yourself to really *own* what you want.

DAVE GIUNTOLI:
CLAIM WHAT YOU REALLY WANT!

In 2003, the actor Dave Giuntoli had finished several seasons appearing on the MTV reality show, "Road Rules." He longed to turn his fifteen minutes of fame into a successful acting career. Dave was humble and hard-working, not the type to make bold declarations (not publicly anyway).

In one of our conversations, I asked, "What do you *really* want?"

He was very pragmatic. "I just need to keep my head down, put in the work, and good things will happen."

While I agreed those were important strengths, he was resisting. His vision was foggy and vague. He was uncomfortable clarifying the big picture of his ultimate desire. I challenged him to clarify his vision so he could move toward it in a more direct way.

"I want to be a working actor in Hollywood."

"No, what do you *really* want?"

There was a long pause. He fidgeted in his chair, visibly uncomfortable. "I want to continue doing this work that I love."

"Dave, if I were a genie in a bottle, and I could grant just one wish, what would that be?"

His eyes rolled. "OK, fine! I want to be the lead actor on a one-hour network series, it could be dramatic or comedic; I don't care. And I want it to run for at least six years, so it goes into syndication."

His tone was sarcastic, as if he didn't really believe it was possible. "Yeah, but what actor doesn't want that?"

"That's not the point. I'm asking *you* to clarify. What others want is irrelevant."

Dave had declared his Big Thing. This shifted his energy. He was no longer just "an actor trying to get work." Rather, he was becoming, "the lead on a network TV series." This changed how he saw himself and shifted his self-identity.

In the coming months, Dave booked several big-budget TV commercials, and then, within two years, landed the lead role as Detective Nick Burkhardt on the NBC hit show, *Grimm*. It aired for more than six years, and is now in syndication. Today, he's staring in the ABC hit series, *A Million Little Things*.

Get as Specific as Possible

People are often clearer than they give themselves credit for. Start by identifying what *is* clear and discount nothing. Then, encourage yourself to get as specific as possible.

CHRIS KLUG:
GO BIG!

Chris sat in my office, speaking of his mission to save lives through organ donation. A former professional snowboarder, he received a liver transplant in 2000 to treat primary sclerosing cholangitis. Chris then went on to compete in the 2002 Winter Olympics in Salt Lake City where he won bronze in the Parallel Giant Slalom. This was the first and only time a transplant recipient had competed in the Olympics.

Chris had been featured on numerous network news programs that highlighted his great work. He had name recognition, and his work was making a difference, but he was uncertain of the exact impact he and his foundation were making.

We delved deeper. He wanted to save lives.

"How many?" I asked.

We researched the national percentage of organ donation

registrations among drivers' license holders. When I first met with Chris, the rate was 40%. He believed that if his foundation could get participation up to 50% nationally, that would work out to about 10 million new organ donations per year. This number broke down to five lives saved every day. In a matter of minutes, we drilled down to a specific Big Thing: "Five lives saved, every day, within three years."

His eyes welled up. Getting specific on his Big Thing made it real, and emotionally palpable. He then declared, "What I *really* want is to eliminate the wait list altogether!"

Boom. That's when the Big Thing solidified. He went from, "Wanting to make the biggest impact humanly possible in organ donation," to, "Eliminating all deaths due to the waitlist for a life-saving transplant by December 1, 2026."

He was so busy in his full life that he'd never slowed down to actually clarify and articulate the specific outcome he most wanted to generate. Many in the organ donation space were deeply inspired, and committed to moving the needle, yet no one had declared they would do this. This is the incredible nature of getting crystal clear on a Big Thing. Clarifying it will change both you and your future.

This immediately boosted fundraising. The Chris Klug Foundation (CKF) was now able to show how dollars given to his organization were going to work to save a specific number of lives each year. Their mission of eliminating deaths due to the wait list was *so* clear and palpable that fundraising was no longer focused on *dollars*. Instead, it concentrated on *lives*.

This led to new ideas and actions that were previously hidden. So far, CKF has signed up 100,000 new app users and massively increased their programming and media exposure. Since that meeting with Chris, their initiatives have contributed to a five percent increase in the national ratio of registered organ donors who have drivers' licenses. This translates to five fewer deaths per day, all year long, surpassing his original milestone.

Chris's desire to use his Big Thing to serve has changed countless lives. The Foundation is one of the most inspired and fun groups of people you could ever hope to meet, and they're on track to realize their ultimate vision. If you're not currently an organ donor, or would like more information, please visit www.ChrisKlugFoundation.org. Being a part of this organization may not only save a life; it may inspire you to define your own Big Thing and go for it.

Clarify your Big Thing and commit to the scope of what you really want. Don't settle for vague outcomes like, "make the greatest difference." Speak it out. Declare it. This takes time and exploration, which is the point of our conversation. Don't expect yourself to fully flesh it out right away. Let it ruminate. While you may have some ideas, it will take time to unfold. That's not only OK, that's good! As you read on, and as more stories unfold, you will start to see clues for yourself. Pay attention to these clues. Be courageous, patient and persistent. If you do, like Chris, you'll speak your Big Thing out loud in no time.

Imagine Not Doing It

In order to fully understand the value of your Big Thing, consider *not* going for it. Imagine five years into your future, having not pursued your Big Thing. Who would you be? How would your life be different?

As I considered whether or not to join the Aconcagua expedition, I imagined who I would be after the climb. I then considered who I would be a year later if I chose *not* to do it. The contrast was night and day. I wanted to become the guy who climbed the mountain, or at least came close, and use every bit of that experience to transform.

Who was "that guy" who went for it? What did *he* learn? Who did *he* become by committing, doing everything required, and playing full out? Even if he didn't reach the summit, who would *that* guy be? I believed he would be courageous, bold, and authentic. I believed the guy who did it would become someone who saw more results in his life than excuses, who walked his talk when he challenged others to go for it. I liked that guy. He is who I really am. He is My Essential Self.

I then considered the guy who *didn't* go for it, the one who said, "I'm not ready. Maybe, someday." Who would I become if I did not say "yes?" Basically, the same guy I was in that moment; a good person, but not a gamechanger. That guy was hesitant, indecisive, pragmatic; my Conditioned Self. He was not who I wanted to be, and not even who I *really* am.

In this way, your Big Thing is a catalyst to immediately spur massive growth. It requires you to change. Going for it will demand you become someone new, someone more equipped to actually see it through. This someone is already latent within you, but only this type of challenge will summon them. This is the transformational power of The Big Thing Effect. It doesn't change you into someone you're not. Rather, it unleashes more of who you already *are*. These old habits and fears have kept you playing small and held you back from letting the tiger out of the cage and taking your true place in the world.

Generate Your "Feeling Fix"

We've focused on clarifying your Big Thing. Now it's time to clarify what you hope to *feel* by realizing it. If you can identify what you want to feel by reaching it, you can begin to cultivate and experience that feeling immediately. I call this your "Feeling Fix."

You say you want more money, but what's the real motivator? You might say, "I want more money so I can take more time off to travel."

I'd ask further, "What will the travel give you?"

You then say, "I would sleep better at night."

I continue, "What would sleeping better do for you?"

Finally, you say, "I'd feel less stress and experience more peace."

Ah, there it is. You can see from our hypothetical conversation how the goal of making more money is really about feeling peace. Knowing this allows you to meet that deeper need with immediacy.

VANESSA:
FINDING HER *FEELING FIX*
SPARKED A MASSIVE BREAKTHROUGH

Vanessa, a tech company founder, came into the office to help improve the presentations she gave at pitch meetings. According to her, she struggled with raising money. As we talked, she uncovered a larger desire to become a more powerful speaker. When I asked her what she hoped to *feel* by achieving that goal, she clearly replied, "I would be *happy*. Accomplishing this goal would make me feel joy."

I asked, "What if you could experience that level of joy right now?"

"Then I would be a better communicator!" she replied. She instantly realized that what was missing from her speaking and business was the quality of *joy*. Minutes before she had been pursuing the perfect presentation, and now she was seeing that what she *really* wanted was to experience more *joy*. Now she was saying that if she were more joyful then her presentations would take care of themselves.

She's absolutely right! What we hope to experience is the *quality* beneath the goal, and when we get in touch with *that*, we bring that richness and vibrancy *to* the goal. And that changes the way we experience our goal, both in the process, and in the outcome. When we approach endeavors in this way, we're less concerned about the outcome because we're enjoying it. The funny thing is that, nine times out of ten, the result is accelerated achievement of the goal with even greater ease.

You might be asking yourself, "How do I do that? How do I touch the quality that I want to experience?"

As I sat with Vanessa, I asked her to think about something she does that brings her joy. With a smile, she replied, "Fly fishing!" I invited her to imagine herself having the best fly-fishing day ever. I encouraged her to describe, in vivid detail, what she might see, feel, touch, and experience. Her face lit up and she began to smile and laugh as she shared her (imagined) perfect day on the river. I asked her to tell me what she was experiencing. She answered, with a smile, "I feel lots of joy."

The amazing thing is that she didn't even leave the office to experience this feeling. I then asked, "If you're feeling joy, then where did it come from?"

She said, "From going fishing."

"But you didn't *go* fishing. You never left the office."

Her eyes sparkled with realization. Fishing helped her access it, but the joy she experienced was already inside. Vanessa began taking small actions every day to cultivate joy. We also elevated her presentation skills to support the pitch meetings.

In less than two months, the frustration was gone. She was having more fun than ever before, and the challenges with raising money had vanished. She completed a middle round of funding for her startup, and, within the year, the company was purchased for a breathtaking valuation.

The Goal Beneath the Goal

Underneath every goal or endeavor that you pursue there is a *quality* that you wish to experience. When you clarify what that quality is, you can access it within yourself. You can begin to cultivate that quality by doing small things that elicit it. You then bring that quality *to* your goals.

Stop falsely thinking that reaching your goal is what will make you happy. Quit seeking fulfillment in achieving, or getting, what you perceive you want. Go straight to the quality you desire *first*. Then use those qualities to fuel your creation of the outcome. In this way, you will not only increase your odds of reaching it, you'll also touch the world with your presence, and radiate those qualities to everyone around you. Doing this will change not only your pursuit of your Big Thing; it will also elevate your life and the lives of those around you.

Exercise:
Generate Your Feeling Fix

An effective way to uncover your Feeling Fix is to imagine yourself in the full expression of your Big Thing, and then notice the dominant feeling (quality of being) that you're experiencing.

Imagine yourself fully experiencing the realization of your Big Thing (and if you don't know your Big Thing yet, use a goal you know is important to you). Picture yourself reaching the summit, receiving the Oscar, or whatever your Big Thing is. Envision it as if it were a film playing out right in front of you. Use your imagination and let the scene come alive with you in the center of it.

What's the dominant quality that you're feeling as you imagine realizing your Big Thing? Is it joy? Perhaps it's a sensation of elation. Maybe it's peace or contentment. It's entirely possible that what you're feeling is so unique that there are no words in your lexicon that perfectly express it. If so, feel free to make up a name for the feeling you're experiencing.

Write down the name of this quality. You may have multiple qualities you're feeling. However, choose the one that's most prominent or the one you most want to feel. This is your Feeling Fix.

Give yourself the Fix that you're yearning for now. When you do, you'll stop holding your breath until the finish line, and start using your Feeling Fix as fuel to reach your Big Thing.

Once you identify the quality you're seeking to experience, ask yourself, "What's one small action I could take, right now, that would elicit that feeling from within, or move me toward it?" Write down as many actions as you can think of, large or small.

Next, highlight one action from this list, and *do it immediately.* Make the cultivation of your Feeling Fix a daily game you play. These actions will swell into a tidal wave of momentum and vibrancy.

You're Closer Than You Think

If you've already clarified your Big Thing, great! If not, I've got your back. Everybody has a Big Thing. *Everybody*. I've yet to meet anyone over 20 years old without one. The challenge is usually giving yourself permission to see it. If you are not totally clear on yours, it's highly possible that you are closer than you realize.

Exercise:
Discovering the Clues to Your Big Thing

Elements of your Big Thing are already at work in your life *right now*. Look for clues right under your nose. Here are a few questions to prompt you:

Write down your answers quickly, without thinking too much.

- What is it that you most want to do at this time?
- What have you always wanted to do, but think it might be impossible or silly?
- Is there a talent or skill you love to express?
- What is it that someone else is doing that makes you envious?
- What do you know you want, but believe you can't have?
- What would you do if you knew you couldn't fail?
- What would you want to do, even if you knew you *would* fail? (Because it would be so much fun that the outcome wouldn't even matter.)
- Who do you want to be in your ideal future?
- Who would you like to spend time with and what would be the nature of your relationship?
- What kind of impact would you have on each other and in the world around you?
- What do you *love* to do (even though you may not be recognized for it)?

76

- What have you been doing for a long time that's just, "part of who you are?"
- What did you dream of doing as a kid?
- What life experiences have been formative for you?

CHAPTER 4

Decide, Declare... Then Fully Commit

GETTING TO "YES"

June 20, 2010 • Glenwood Springs, Colorado

Having just written down the vision of what I truly hoped the Aconcagua expedition would become, I was getting in touch with the real juice of the opportunity. Filled with excitement and unable to get back to sleep, I got out of bed and went downstairs to make some tea. I turned the flame on under the kettle, and as the water heated up, so did my imagination. I could begin to see what life might look like during, and *after,* the climb. It's difficult to make such a big decision if you can't see the outcome.

When I could imagine myself standing on the summit, the decision became clearer, even though I had no idea how I would actually see it through. It would change *everything:* my relationships, my business, and my contribution in the world.

This also helped me realize what I'd been avoiding. I was delaying making a decision about a vision this big because I was paying more attention to the doubts, fears, and false beliefs that said I wasn't ready. I'd been hypnotized by my own habits into assuming this wasn't me.

This expedition was more than simply accomplishing a feat I'd envisioned since I was a boy. The real quest was who I would become as a result. By writing down the vision of what I wanted this to culminate into, I began to see what was possible. No longer solely focused on what it would cost, I was now fixed on what would occur. I could see it so clearly that I could taste it. When I looked at that possibility, it was clear. I said "yes." This was my next Big Thing.

I managed to hold back my excitement another three hours, until the minimally socially acceptable hour of 7:00 a.m., when I called Stephen to share my decision.

Decide and Declare

Once you get clear on your Big Thing, it's time to say an official "yes." Draw a line in the sand and step over it. This acknowledges that you're no longer confused. No longer flipping and flopping. You've decided.

Once you do, don't hide in the shadows. Declare it. By saying it out loud, you're allowing the world around you to support you in your vision and hold you accountable. It will also allow something incredible to start happening immediately. When you decide and declare your Big Thing, the universe rises up to meet you, and you start to experience synchronicities that you couldn't have orchestrated with your own mind if you'd tried.

COPPER MOUNTAIN:
DECLARING IGNITES MAGIC

Twenty years ago, when I was living in Los Angeles, I made a list of 100 things I wanted to do in my life. They ranged from large to small. At the very top of the list was, "Snow skiing in the mountains."

I decided to take one item from that list and *do* it. I circled "snow skiing" and began future-visioning my ideal ski trip. I pulled out my journal and began writing.

The first words on the page were, "I'm going skiing! I'm in the Rocky Mountains, on a ski lift, as the sun warms my face…" I continued to describe the very best ski trip I could imagine. It was five days, with epic skiing, surrounded by fun people. All was taken care of, and I could easily afford it.

Just then the phone rang. My good friend Mike chirped, "Jeffy, what are you doing?"

"I'm going skiing!" It popped out. I couldn't believe what I was saying because I had no money, no skis, and no clue how this was going to happen.

"Where are you going?" Mike asked.

"I don't know," I said, "but I have a gig in Denver the first weekend in March, and I'd like to go after that."

Mike said, "I'll call you right back."

I went back to my journal and continued future-visioning this ski trip. I imagined riding the lift with new friends, laughing on the slopes, and having dinner and drinks with a group at a cozy lodge. I was having so much fun writing this vision because it felt like it was happening.

The phone rang again, and before I could say, "Hello" Mike yelled, "You're all set! My cousin works at Copper Mountain and she can get you no-charge lift tickets, ski rentals, and you can stay with her friends. She also works at a restaurant and has vouchers for you. Everything's taken care of. All you have to do is get there."

I was blown away, then wondered, "How in the world *do* I get there?" I thanked Mike profusely, and went back to the journal. I continued writing, but now I had some facts to weave in. I wrote about how I was driving a clean, new car up to the resort, and, I kid you not, the phone rang again. This time, it was Brian Abell, the producer, with the travel arrangements for the Nickelodeon game show we were hosting at the Pepsi Center.

After asking what I was up to, I said, "I'm going skiing," and told him about how Mike had set me up at Copper Mountain. Then he asked how I was going to get from Denver to the ski resort (which was about a 90-minute drive).

"I'm not clear on that part yet."

Brian said, "Jeff, I know *exactly* how you're going to get there. After the show, take the rental car from the production."

I sheepishly confessed that I didn't have the cash to cover the car rental for five extra days. He quickly admonished me for even suggesting I should pay.

"Don't be silly! It will be our birthday present to you for doing such a fantastic job hosting the show."

There it was. Within 30 minutes of *deciding and declaring* that I was going skiing, out of nowhere, I was set for a five-day trip, all expenses paid.

When you get crystal clear about what you want, and you *choose* to create it, and then declare it ("I'm going skiing") even if you don't know how, the magic happens. Perhaps, in your life, you've gotten excited to do something, but when you met opposition, you lost confidence and the initiative fizzled. This is likely because you hadn't *fully* committed. Instead, you tried to figure out *how* before you could go "all in." Unfortunately, this can derail even the best of endeavors. Decide and declare, *then* plot out the how.

Fully Commit

Many people think once they've decided and declared their Big Thing, that they've fully committed, but they haven't. Without true commitment, your decision and declaration will remain merely a vision in your journal.

Intention vs. Commitment

There's an important distinction between your *intention* and *commitment*. You may decide that you're going to do something, and even tell someone you're going to do it, but if something comes up, you might not. This kind of decision is only living at the level of intention.

An intention is an idea of something you *plan* to do. Intentions are great and powerful. You might intend to work out today, and by intending it, you stand a greater chance of doing it than if you hadn't clearly set that intention, but because it's merely an intention, it's easy to derail.

By contrast, a commitment is a declaration of what we will *actually* do, not merely intend to do. You're putting a stake in the ground. With a commitment, there's no wiggle room. It states, "I *will* do this by this date." It's powerful, clear, and will require something more of you than merely an intention. A commitment is a stance that you come *from*. It's about how you will operate. It's active, and you will have to adjust how you show up to support your decision to do the thing you've committed to do.

There are moments when it makes sense to set an intention, but taking on your Big Thing isn't one of them. Your Big Thing requires fully committing in no uncertain terms.

I'M ALL IN
June 1, 2010 • Aconcagua Training Begins

I'd said "yes," and I'd told Stephen. Now came the hard part—actually doing the work. Fully showing up. Joining the Aconcagua expedition required commitment on many levels. The first was financial. The $10,000 deposit was due in ten days, and I was struggling to come up with it.

That's when the Big Thing Effect kicked in. To raise the funds, I decided to start a group-coaching program for ten people, something I'd secretly thought I wasn't ready to do. It filled up in two weeks.

Upping the ante on this commitment spilled over into the business. It just sort of happened. It didn't seem extraordinary until *after* the group was full. The result was significantly more than I needed for the deposit. It was a major boost in my overall business and confidence.

I raised my fees and was forced to up my game on many fronts. This is something I had intended to do for years. Yet it took a commitment to turn that intention into reality. A commitment is not solely a declaration of what you will *do*. It's also a declaration of who you will *be* as you move toward the destination. A true commitment implies that you will shift who you're being if that's what's required to do what you said you would do, even if that means being someone you didn't think possible. This is one of the transformational aspects of commitment.

It took several months, but I accomplished the thing I had

thought impossible. Not only did I raise the $10,000 for the deposit, but I generated the full $50,000 for the entire expedition, double my prior year's income.

Restructuring Life Around the Training

Joining the Aconcagua expedition also required a number of important training commitments. The first were two mandatory team workouts each week in Denver (a three-and-a-half-hour drive from my home near Aspen). This meant two of my weekdays were now being devoted to training and travel. This was in addition to daily workouts at home. I was pushing my mind and body in ways I hadn't done in decades. Each week, I spent more than twenty-seven hours training, not counting the ten trips to Denver each month. In addition to the regular strength and conditioning training, we were also committing to participate in monthly team-training climbs on 14,000-foot peaks.

This level of commitment couldn't just "fit into" my life. I had to restructure life around the commitment. Clients had to be rescheduled. Lindsay and I had to change when we spent quality time together, the kind of food we ate, and the time we went to bed, all because of the training schedule. I had to forgo fishing weekends and visiting family. This is the meaning of true commitment. The irony of making this level of commitment to my Big Thing is that it had me showing up so much more intentionally and focused for all those other areas of my life.

Build Your World Around it

If you're serious about realizing your Big Thing, build your world around it, rather than trying to squeeze it into your already busy life.

HE PASSED UP A SURE THING
FOR A SHOT AT HIS BIG THING

In 1998, I was hosting "Totally Nickelodeon at Universal Studios, Hollywood." As I stood in the dressing room, I looked at my reflection in the mirror framed by bright, clear bulbs, and massaged sculpting paste into my spikey hair. There was a knock at the door as the Stage Manager yelled, "Thirty minutes to showtime!" My stomach dropped, as it did before every show. Suddenly, my co-host burst through the door with a look of panic on his face.

"I have a problem. I just got offered *Smokey Joe's Café* on Broadway."

I was confused. "But that's one of your dreams, how is that a prob–"

"Because I have to leave Los Angeles in two days to go to New York for the next six months, which means I can't audition for Pilot Season." He was in visible pain.

Pilot Season is the three months between February and April during which new shows are pitched in Hollywood. He'd have to leave LA and give up even the chance of landing a new pilot. He had to choose between taking a sure thing and stepping back from his Big Thing.

He winced, asking, "What do you think I should do?"

The bass of pre-show music thumped through the walls of the dressing room. I asked him to state his ultimate goal, even though I knew the answer.

"I want to be the next Flip Wilson and star on a variety show like *Laugh-In*."

Talk about a Big Thing! By the way, this was not the sort of thing he shared publicly. My friend was very earnest and hardworking and wasn't the kind of person to boast about his dreams.

I offered, "Imagine that you're five years in the future, and *see* yourself in the full expression of the success you desire. *See* yourself on network TV." I went further, "Now, focus on you; the *future* you; who you are. Not just what you're *doing*, but who that guy is *being*."

His eyes closed and his face lit up.

"Good!" I said. "Now, tell me what *he* would do in this situation?"

He opened his eyes and whispered, "I know what I've got to do."

His manager was livid. His friends thought he was crazy. He stayed in L.A.

Within a few months, he landed a small role in a pilot for VH-1 called *Vinyl Justice*. In the months that followed, a producer from England was bringing a successful show from Britain to ABC, and he happened to see the *Vinyl Justice* pilot.

The producer brought my co-host in to audition, then brought him back for network testing. They decided to take a chance on an unknown. Six months later, my co-host became a household name: Wayne Brady, from *Who's Line Is It Anyway?*

Many people go for the sure thing. Wayne did the opposite. He turned down a *sure* thing, a dream job and better money, *for the chance* at his Big Thing. Even more, he was willing to build his world *around* his Big Thing, rather than fitting it into his already busy life. He had moved from Florida to Las Vegas, then Los Angeles in 1996, to work in theater and television. He'd been working toward this for more than a decade.

Make your Big Thing important. When faced with a similar decision, what would you do?

Self-Created Urgency

Have you made your Big Thing *urgent?* Many people make everything on their to-do list critical, but if everything is urgent, then nothing can be urgent. Something becomes pressing because you say so. All urgency is self-created, but many people falsely believe their circumstances determine their priorities.

SANDY HESSLER: CIRCUMSTANCES DON'T DECIDE WHAT IS URGENT

Sandy, a former Assistant Dean at the Harvard Kennedy School of Government, was writing her book and hoping to create a weekly blog. She complained of not being able to write consistently. She said she, "didn't have the discipline at the moment."

I challenged her, saying that she was not lacking discipline, but rather, commitment. I suggested that she was not making her writing *urgent*. She thoughtfully pushed back saying, because of other important responsibilities, she was unable to make it urgent.

Together we explored the idea of urgency. I had her contemplate the possibility that urgency is not something that happens *to* you, but rather is something you decide.

I reflected back on a powerful moment from her past. A few years earlier, Sandy's husband had been diagnosed with brain cancer, and the prognosis was dire. Upon hearing this news, she quit her prestigious job, risked sabotaging her career, became her husband's fierce advocate, and moved their family of six from Boston to the Teton Mountains of Wyoming.

I asked, "Sandy, how did you come to that decision at the time?"

She said, "It wasn't my decision. It needed to be done. Life decided *for* me."

Sandy was so determined to give her husband and children what they needed to heal, that, for her, there was no other option, but life didn't force her to decide to make his health urgent. She did. This took enormous courage, although she didn't see it that way at the time. She gave all the power to the circumstance, rather than seeing that she actually *created* the urgency. Yes, circumstances motivated her, but, ultimately, she was the one to make the decision urgent and then act on that urgency.

Seeing that moment from new perspective, she reclaimed the power she was giving away. Sandy quickly saw that she could do the same with her new book, and, seven months later, she had a manuscript.

Life and circumstances don't decide what's urgent. You do. Reclaim this power and don't give it away to outside forces. Gamechangers determine their own urgency.

Sandy's husband recovered from cancer and is joyfully living today, and all her children are thriving young adults.

Go All the Way with Your Word

Perhaps one of the biggest gifts in training for Aconcagua was my decision to bring urgency to my agreements. This meant fulfilling *every* promise I made to myself, and the team, no matter what. To a part of me, this felt extreme. It seemed rigid. I mean, what if circumstances changed that kept me from fulfilling a promise? Or what if a situation changed and what I promised was no longer relevant?

Regardless of my fears, I chose to play this way because for much of my life, I'd grown comfortable with excuses and reasons for not having what I wanted. This expedition was a test that I was putting myself through, "What might happen if I actually do everything I say I will, with no exceptions?"

HONORING MY WORD GAVE ME POWER
November 22, 2010
Aconcagua Training • Glenwood Springs, Colorado

The alarm chimed. I squinted at the digits and hit snooze. It was 3:30 a.m.

I thought, *Do I* really *have to drive three hours to Denver for the Aconcagua Team workout? I could miss one. I'm so tired. What if I fall asleep at the wheel?*

I looked out the window at four inches of new snow. Surely the team would understand.

At 3:40 the alarm chimed again. I didn't want to go, and I frankly feared it might be unwise to brave the roads. I didn't know what to do, but washed my face and put on workout clothes. I felt frustrated. *Is this what I signed up for?*

Scraping ice off the windshield, I cursed under my breath. *Whose idea was this anyway?!* My thoughts were focused on the warm bed in the house rather than the snow packed roads on Vail Pass. Reluctantly, I buckled up and pulled onto the highway, resolved to turn around if it became too dangerous.

Six hours later, we completed the exhausting two-hour workout at Red Rocks Park led by our trainer and fellow team member, Eric Wiseman. This included pushups, pullups, and burpees in full winter gear with weighted packs. We ran sprints up the stairs of the amphitheater, 138 steps to the top, and then bear-crawled to the bottom. Many times.

On the drive home, I reflected on how my day might have transpired had I stayed in bed, honoring the voice that said, "I could miss just one." As I did so, I felt lethargic. I could feel the shame at the idea of not honoring my agreement. That feeling was familiar. For much of my past, I let myself off the hook with commitments when it seemed *reasonable*. No one else observed it, but I knew.

As I drove over the peaks, a smile overcame me. I began reviewing the events of the day and how, this time, I showed up differently. I stepped into a new way of operating as it related to my word. I went *all the way*. An indescribable sensation of wholeness and esteem emerged. I felt a sense of satisfaction, as if to say, "I deserve to be here."

I wasn't extraordinary at any point of that day, but I can tell you that my choice to do what I *said* I would do had me *feeling* extraordinary. I felt like a pillar, a post, a mountain!

For some reason, I had always associated commitment with moral rightness. Keeping promises was something you *should* do. If I didn't, it meant that I was a bad person. Consequently, I'd beat myself up when I fell short or didn't do as promised, which didn't really help change the behavior.

But what I experienced that day is that following through (all the way, 100%) feels really good. It may not feel good as we do it, but when we complete it, we're left with an inner sensation of wholeness. On that day, I felt congruency.

Don't follow through just because it's "right." Follow through because it will have you being filled with esteem. Do so selfishly because it feels good.

Broken Commitments Drain Energy

If you want a surefire way to deplete your energy and undermine your self-esteem, start breaking agreements with yourself and with others. Simply don't do what you promised.

Where there's a broken agreement, there's a leak. Every time I break an agreement it causes a tiny rupture inside my energy field that bleeds vital energy. The more I don't do what I said I'd do, the more leaks spring. And the more leaks there are, the more depleted I get, and the less I trust myself.

The issue with these leaks is that they don't only affect the area where the agreement is broken. They are affecting every area of life. It's important that you plug them, or they'll run you down until you don't even have the energy to see something's amiss.

DR. BRIAN:
RESTORING POWER TO YOUR WORD

Recently, I was coaching a doctor from NYC who was struggling to build his private practice. This was a very successful person, yet he had a rough year financially.

At the last minute, he asked to reschedule our first meeting due to "fires" he had to put out. For the second meeting, he showed up five minutes late. When we finally sat down, I reflected that he had already broken two agreements before we even met. I had no judgment about this and wasn't saying it to make him feel bad.

I asked if I could show him something. He agreed, and we walked out to the parking lot. There I lifted an empty plastic gallon jug. I said, "Let's pretend this jug is you, and every time you make an agreement, we add a cup of water into the jug."

"I'll be home at 6:00." (I poured some water into the jug.)

"I'll call you back in ten minutes." (I poured more water into the jug.)

"I'll fix the leaky faucet this week." (I poured more water into the jug.)

"Get the idea?" I asked. He nodded.

"Now, what happens to the jug (you) when you *don't* follow through on what you agreed to do?"

He searched for an answer, "I don't know."

I pulled out a ballpoint pen and punched a hole in the jug. It started to squirt. I asked, "When you break your word, what happens?"

"There's a leak."

"Yes. And what happens when you break another agreement?"

He smiled, "It starts another leak."

I handed him the pen and told him to punch a hole in the jug for every agreement he had broken that week. He jabbed the jug again and again. Water was squirting everywhere.

Finally, I asked, "If this jug were you, what's happening?"

With tears rolling down his face, he said, "I'm being drained."

Every time we break an agreement, be it with ourselves, or another, we spring a leak in our own energy. The more you break them, the more you deplete your energy, esteem, and trust in yourself.

How do you plug a leak?

First, acknowledge that you didn't do what you said you would do, when you said you would do it. Be honest. Excuses and rationalizations have no place in this conversation because they don't matter. An agreement is kept or it's broken, regardless of any reasons or excuses.

Second, clean up any mess that your broken agreement may have produced by taking 100% responsibility, making amends, and taking a course of corrective action. Doing this will plug the leak and restore your energy.

After illustrating the impact of broken commitments with the doctor, he saw a leak he could plug, namely following up on receivables for his practice. He agreed to plug that leak by the end of the week. At 5:00 p.m. on Friday, he called to say he had done so and deposited $40,000 into his bank account.

Most important was his voice, which sounded alive and clear, as if a weight had been lifted from his shoulders.

ELIAS:
HOLDING OTHERS TO THEIR WORD IS AS IMPORTANT AS KEEPING YOUR OWN

A few years ago, I was coaching Elias, the CEO of an East Coast real estate firm. He kept saying he was fatigued and approaching retirement. In one of our sessions, Elias brought up a longstanding agreement with a business partner that he had not honored. As it turned out, Elias was not holding his business associate accountable for an overdue payment. Because Elias cared about his partner and was aware of the challenges this associate faced financially, he ignored the agreement they had made.

I encouraged Elias to start by acknowledging the agreement and him not honoring it. I challenged him to see that he was out of integrity by not admitting it and initiating a clean-up. You may think it's the person who made the promise who's solely on the hook. Not true. You're both giving your word in the agreement. If one of you learns that the other is not honoring it, it's up to you to bring it forward. This will maintain integrity for you both.

Another reason Elias resisted addressing this situation was because he didn't see what could be done about the cleanup. Because he didn't have the solution, he didn't want to irritate a sensitive area. He hoped it would resolve itself, but it didn't.

I confronted him to address it, and eventually clean it up. He met the challenge with courage and care. It was a little uncomfortable at first, but he negotiated a new agreement with the partner. This was an enormous relief for both of them because they were now addressing the leak that had produced tension for everyone.

This is what happens when you honor your word, even when you break promises. You honor your word by acknowledging your broken promise and then cleaning it up. Doing so restores your integrity, which replenishes your power. This is a hidden factor to confidence that many people don't realize.

Elias felt a burst of confidence that led him to look at *all* his broken agreements. He quickly started noticing other places in his life where he had not kept his word, and because he had worked through the uncomfortable clean-up of the partnership, he had the courage to tackle *all* those broken promises, including losing 30 pounds. After years of not taking that promise seriously, he committed.

This created a huge shift for Elias. He dropped the weight and started feeling younger and more alive than ever. Instead of deciding to retire, he chose to stay on and lead the company through a complicated merger.

By plugging his leaks, he increased his professional esteem and confidence. This helped him set his sights on a much larger goal. As he entered this new phase, he realized that this new challenge was something he'd actually wanted for a long time, but hadn't identified. Who he became (lighter, leaner, stronger) made a real and lasting impact.

Elias's inspired presence and leadership led to a successful merger which resulted in the company becoming a billion-dollar frontrunner in their market. More importantly, Elias was on fire with enthusiasm and said he enjoyed one of the best years of his professional life.

Creating Consequences Holds You Accountable

In a linear existence, each day affects the next. Action has consequence. So does inaction. People often ask, "Why don't we do the things we know we need to do?"

The answer is simple. We don't immediately feel the consequences. We put off going to the dentist. We skip exercise. We don't take time for meditation. We don't do it because we don't yet feel the pain of *not* doing it today. If we put it off, it won't be a big deal. It may be a tender spot right now, but the cumulative affect over time is tremendous.

Often clients acknowledge they have something they need

to do, something that would make a huge difference, and they're not doing it. There are all kinds of ways to create leverage to help yourself over the hump to get something done. In some instances, people will impose a short-term consequence if they don't, something painful, so they feel the immediacy in a way they can't put off. They stop thinking inaction won't hurt.

BEVERLY:
CREATING A CONSEQUENCE
GAVE HER LEVERAGE

I was coaching Beverly and her adult family as a group. Beverly had always wanted to meditate for thirty days straight. She struggled with anxiety and yearned to feel a deepened sense of calm. She tried many programs and wished to be consistent in her meditation practice. For more than a decade she was unable to do it. This is someone who was very accomplished in business, from a very successful family, yet she didn't understand why she didn't meditate.

She said, "I can't bring myself to do it."

I asked, "Well, what's the consequence if you don't?"

(Crickets). She stared at her shoes.

"What would be the most awful consequence, the most uncomfortable thing you can think of for yourself in the event that you don't meditate every day? What consequence are you willing to follow through on?"

In front of her husband and four adult children, she said, "I'll get my initials tattooed on my right butt cheek."

We both started laughing.

Doing this would not only have been painful to her, but also extremely psychologically uncomfortable.

Thirty-one days later she was high-fiving her family in tears because she'd finally done it. Once she had set an immediate consequence, she was able to do the thing she had not been able to do for more than a decade. She sat still for twenty minutes, every day, for a month.

Inner Commitment

Go beyond intention and put yourself on the hook. Commit fully and build your world around your Big Thing. Make promises and follow through, even if you're nervous or concerned you can't live up to it. Go to great lengths to do it anyway. If you fall short, acknowledge it and clean it up. Relating to your word with this level of follow-through is in-credible—it creates credibility within. This results in a feeling of esteem that's as powerful as the action itself. Most of all, a commitment isn't merely a statement of where you're going. Rather, it's a declaration of where you're coming from. Operating in this manner will not only transform your results, it will transform your life.

CHAPTER 5

Focus on the Moment

ONE STEP AT A TIME
AND EVERYTHING'S FINE

September 15, 2010
Training Climb • Longs Peak, Colorado

We left the trailhead at 5:00 a.m. in hopes of reaching the summit by noon. At 14,259 feet, Longs is one of Colorado's highest peaks. By 8:00 o'clock, the September sunrise warmed our backs as the summit began to sparkle above us. It was majestic, like a scene out of a movie. The combo of morning coffee and camaraderie accelerated the pace.

Just as we cleared timberline and emerged in the Boulder Field, I suddenly felt a twinge in my right knee. *Damn it, no!* During a training a few months ago, I had injured my IT band. To heal it, I'd made weekly trips to Boulder for a month for physical therapy, including dry needling and the most painful "massages" (myofascial release) I'd ever endured. I'd thought it was fixed.

I slowed down to stretch, and encouraged the guys to keep going, promising to catch up. With some stretching the sensation was bearable. I hustled to rejoin the team. A few hours later, the twinge escalated to discomfort, and then into sharp pain. I was still trailing behind.

At some point, teammate Eric Wiseman came back to join me. Feebly attempting small talk, I asked if he'd seen how beautiful the summit looked in the clear morning sky.

He agreed but quickly paused with look of concern. "We've

got a ways to go before the top. It might be helpful to take your focus off the summit and place it onto the next small thing you need to do."

It may sound simple at sea level, but I'm telling you, at the time, given the pain I was in and the vertical distance we still needed to climb, this felt like a rope thrown to a drowning man.

I asked myself: *What's the next thing I need to do?* In that moment, it was stretching and hydrating. So, that became my summit—my entire reason for being on this training climb. I focused on this simple activity with all the will I could muster. I was no longer thinking about whether or not I would make it to the top. Rather, I focused on my outstretched leg and the water bottle against my lips until I was able to climb again. To help strengthen my focus, I created a phrase and began repeating it: "One step at a time and everything's fine." This became part of my rhythm and it helped me to settle down and keep moving forward.

Eric and I continued climbing up the Boulder Field until we reached the rest of the team who were sitting at the entrance to the Keyhole, a narrow passage you must crawl through to continue on up to the summit. I asked why they had stopped, but before they had a chance to answer, a park ranger approached. In a gravelly voice, he announced, "Guys, we're going to ask you to hold here for thirty minutes. There's been a fatality on the mountain, and we're preparing to extract the body."

If the knee pain hadn't woken me up during the four-and-a-half hour climb to the Keyhole, this news sure did. We looked at each other without a word. Having never climbed Longs Peak before, I had no idea what lay ahead on the push to the summit. Now, with the news of a man falling to his death, my mind had ideas other than summiting.

I was debating if I should turn around and head down the mountain, but decided to get a look at what we were about to climb next. I crawled up into the Keyhole, squeezed through the small passageway, and looked at the next section called The Narrows, a twelve-inch-wide lip of granite that you must traverse for twenty yards with nothing to hold onto. I looked down over the edge. BIG mistake.

My eyes strained to see the scree field some 2,000 feet below. My stomach dropped. *I'm out. I'm done. I can't do this!* My eyes welled with tears. I felt like a four-year-old, and wanted to be held by my mommy.

The air became thick. Each breath was a struggle. The sound of my breathing was so loud in my head that everything else was muffled. My chest tightened and lungs burned as I crawled back out of the Keyhole and collapsed on the rocks, gasping for air. Sweating profusely, my body was having its own reaction, and I was at its mercy. This was a full-on panic attack. The guys looked at me wide-eyed.

First the knee and now *this? What was I thinking? I'm terrified of heights! Did I think the acrophobia would magically disappear?* I was questioning everything, and, most of all, my sanity for saying "yes" to this expedition. If this training climb was too much, what in the world would I do on Aconcagua? I searched for any excuse that I could give the team to turn back. Death seemed the perfect reason to retreat.

Eric put his hand on my shoulder and reminded me of my mantra. Trying to regain some shred of composure, I repeated, "One step at a time and everything's fine." However, one step felt like a mountain at this point. I needed to alter my mantra to, "One *breath* at a time and everything's fine." I focused on my breath, the sensations in my body, and this phrase, trying to put the exposed drop-off out of my mind.

What this situation prompted was slowing down and getting still with my own feelings and fears that had been running below the surface. This delay forced me to experience my own inner climate. This was the first time I'd actually ever *felt* these feelings when faced with my fear of heights, instead of trying to ignore or push past them. This time, with each breath, the sensation of terror began to dissipate. After thirty minutes of this practice, the fear turned to calm.

"All right guys, it's clear to move ahead." The ranger's gruff voice pulled me out of my reverie and I opened my eyes. "Just be aware that a chopper will be extracting the body as you climb."

Given my newfound inner calm, I decided to proceed, and, one-by-one, we each crawled through the Keyhole and gingerly inched our way across The Narrows. Being so exposed on this ledge, my hands began to shake. To calm myself again, I breathed deeply and slowly, and repeated the phrase, *one step at a time, and everything's fine.*

"You've got this Jeff," Stephen reassuringly called out from behind.

I was so grateful to be surrounded by caring teammates. I could never have done this on my own.

As we passed over The Narrows, we heard the helicopter approach and settle into a hover over the dead climber. The propwash was kicking up dirt. A long cable lowered the rescue basket down to the ranger. We clung to the wall as the ranger below rolled the black body bag into the basket and waved off the pilot.

As the basket ascended, I feared this was a sign. Was this foreshadowing my future? An overwhelming impulse to turn back overcame me. I couldn't take my eyes off the body dangling in the sky. Who was he? Who was he leaving behind? What had his life been like?

It was a tangible lesson in focusing on where I wanted to go, not on where I didn't. My mind was a hurricane, and it was all I could do to keep climbing, one step at a time. It's amazing how present you get when you come face-to-face with death. That's why adrenaline junkies love this. It puts you so present in the moment that there's no time for anything but the exact thing you are doing.

We finally made it to the top and stood on the summit. Everyone was grinning and wiping away tears. We were hugging and laughing and bawling like babies. I saw something in their eyes I'd never seen so fully. I saw their soul. They were completely present. They were absolutely alive. Maybe that's because *I* was more present and alive than ever.

Taking focus off the summit and placing it on the next rock in front helped me to stay present. It grounded me in a way that I'd never experienced so fully. It also showed me a way to work through fear, which allowed me to keep going where, in the past, I'd have surely tapped out.

Think Small to Go Big

As you move from the commitment stage, it's important that you shift your focus from the outcome of your summit to the next step right in front of you. Most people think the next step they need is a comprehensive plan. You might have a plan, and it may come together organically, like if you're training for a marathon, but in some instances, you may not need one. The plan is simply to identify the next small step, and take it.

Most people have an idea of what they want to do, and they rush into the how. As we discussed earlier, when the vision is clear, the resources appear. The how is one resource that starts crystalizing when you're clear on the what. For now, just take the next small action. Don't over-think it. Just move forward. The creation of a detailed plan is a conversation for another day.

There are two kinds of actions: micro and macro. As the name implies, micro actions are tiny. They're so small they require no other action in order to perform them.

A macro action is bigger. It may require some courage.

A macro action might be booking a trip to Argentina. Or maybe setting up an appointment with the founders of the private equity fund to pitch them on your new app. Or having the conversation with your lover expressing what's not working and what you're committed to in your relationship. A macro action requires a series of micro actions to be taken first.

The micro actions that support the trip to Argentina, for example, might be looking up the flight information, or putting dates on the calendar. A micro action that supports the private equity meeting might be looking up an email address or getting the name of an assistant.

Often, when we're stuck, it's because we're thinking too *big*.

Start small and knock some little tasks down like dominoes, until momentum starts to build.

A fun little game to play is asking this question: "What's one macro action that would move me toward my Big Thing?" Write it down.

Then ask, "What's one *micro* action I could take *today* that will move me closer to my macro action?" Listen, and you will hear your answer within. You'll likely identify a lot of micro actions you could take.

Now ask, "Am I *willing* to take it?" Action is kryptonite to resistance. Change your state. Do some jumping jacks. Get your blood moving. Shift your energy. Yell out loud. Then take one small action. Repeat.

By taking micro actions daily you will be knocking out macro actions every few days or so. Pop the micros like daily vitamins and pat yourself on the back for them. As you build momentum, you'll naturally feel more confident to start taking bigger steps. This is The Big Thing Effect in action.

If you're not clear on your Big Thing yet, that's fine. If that's the case, then ask, "What's one small step I can take toward *clarifying* my Big Thing?" Clarifying your Big Thing can be just as important and urgent as pursuing it. Start right now, making a list of micro actions you could take toward clarifying your Big Thing. For example, re-read Chapter 1, complete the exercises, go to www.TheBigThingEffect.com/resources and listen to one of the guided visualization exercises.

Keep this list with you, and cross off a few each day. Get into a groove of knocking small ones off the list. Then take some chances. And, because of the work you've done in this book, your actions will be humming with new vibrancy. Hold on tight, because you're in for a great ride.

Remove Distractions

Once you commit to your Big Thing, one of the first actions to consider is to remove any distractions that may be in the way of your full participation—distractions like, "I must urgently update my Facebook page"; "the lawn needs mowing *right now*"; or "it's time to reorganize my office."

A few months ago, I had a spirited conversation with a young man in his twenties. He had cut himself off from the social media that he usually indulged in, and said something very insightful: "We must have twice the drive to push through all the distraction that social media hurls at us."

His statement reminded me of my early days of coaching. Many friends, and even well-meaning family, encouraged me to read the newspapers and stay informed. I remember a conversation when my Dad admonished me, "You need to be aware of what the Yuan is doing in China."

I do? I felt like a child. Maybe he was right. Maybe I should be up on social media, reading about all the ramifications of current events.

I subscribed to the *Wall Street Journal.* I thought, *That will do it.* With feeble enthusiasm, I started following global politics. It wasn't long before I felt a connection to my peers. At the same time, I also felt disconnected from my purpose, from my mission, and living fully into it. While I did want to be informed, I didn't have the bandwidth to read about everything going on in the world. I needed to be more vigilant about *my* world, *my* Big Thing. After 30 days, I decided I would take my chances by putting my Big Thing above being informed. I canceled my subscription and refocused on my dream with reckless abandon, leaving politics to the pundits.

Today I'm more informed than I was fifteen years ago (though I'm still not sure I can tell you what the Yuan is doing off the top of my head). I do see it as a civic duty to be aware of what's going on in the world, but I'm grateful for my stubborn focus at the time, refusing to get sucked into the media machine. Due to the growth in my business and family, I'm now able to engage in those activities with a finer balance. Now that I'm living fully into my life's mission, I can watch the news and not let it pull me from center. Nothing will keep me from forging ahead in the direction of my true purpose. Nothing.

It's convenient to use the state of the world as an excuse to back off and say, "Why bother if the world is falling apart?" It's distraction.

Your Big Thing is more important than Facebook, pop culture, or world affairs. The news is already history. I'd rather *make* headlines than read them. Aren't you more interested in creating what's next?

Sure, stay informed. Stand up for what's right, but if that becomes a convenient distraction from being the activist for your own dream, then be cautious of your motive. Is your behavior about being informed, or is it resistance to clarifying, committing to, and going for your Big Thing?

Small Distractions Can Make a Big Impact

Sometimes we get complacent with a minor distraction and then it becomes the norm and we don't even see it.

THE PEBBLE IN MY SHOE

One morning, I stepped out for a walk with Bailey, our black Lab. As we strolled along the bike path skirting the mountains, I felt a small pebble in my shoe. It was so small that I shrugged and kept walking. Fifteen minutes later, I could feel the pebble nestling under the ball of my foot. I wasn't in pain but it was annoying.

I thought about stopping to take off the shoe. Was it worth the trouble? I'd have to untie and then retie it. Bailey might sit while she watched me, but what would it take to get her old hips up and moving again? After ten minutes, I was already mentally fatigued. I'd spent ten minutes considering if it was prudent when it would have taken about thirty seconds to pop off the shoe and resolve the issue. What insight might have come to mind had I not been distracted by the pebble or my internal dialogue about it?

I stopped and removed the pebble from my shoe.

As I observed this comedy, I wondered how I might apply

this metaphor to my training for Aconcagua. What was the pebble in my shoe? Where was I tolerating something that seemed innocuous yet might really be a distraction?

The immediate answer was *sugar*. I'd always had a sweet tooth, and because I've always been slender, this never seemed like a health issue. However, like an addict, I found myself interrupting my day for a sweet treat, often obsessing about where it would come from. That's one of the markers of addiction. As I thought about it, it occupied my mind more than I wanted to confess. I wasn't asserting dominion over this behavior. It was a habit, and it was gaining an unhealthy prominence.

I considered what life might be like if this sugar habit were replaced by something else. I knew that if I kicked sugar, then I would replace it with enhanced focus and trust in myself. No one else could have seen that as a possibility.

The Fear that Your Big Thing Will Derail Your Life

One distraction that affects many people is the fear that the extra energy and time devoted to their Big Thing will derail their current life. However, in most instances, the opposite is true. The energy and vitality from pursuing this endeavor starts elevating other areas of your life. This is part of The Big Thing Effect.

DR. NICOLA SISO:
THE UNEXPECTED OUTCOME
FROM HER BIG THING

Dr. Nicola Siso had been working for several years on a very important arm of her business, coaching those with Type 1 diabetes. She had worked through her own challenges with the disease, and wanted to help others find the relief and healing she had experienced through natural protocols. She believed this was her Big Thing.

Dr. Nicola had also struggled with a persistent habit of smoking marijuana. She didn't feel out of control, but she was not able to shake the habit. She explained that this was also one of the goals she wanted to accomplish in our working together. I made it explicitly clear that I was not an addiction specialist, and that I couldn't guarantee such an outcome, but I did explain how uncovering your Big Thing can change your life, such that other issues you may be dealing with also get handled.

As I began coaching her to create and launch her programs, something felt off, and I shared this with her during one of her sessions. I also shared that an image kept popping into my mind of her in a TV studio hosting a show. She got very quiet. Her stare was intense, and then tears began to well. She confided that this was what she had always wanted. She hadn't told anyone and had even forgotten this dream herself.

"That's it." She said, "That's what I want to do."

We explored further, and she said, "What I *really* want is to become the Oprah of health." As you might imagine, she was lit up. She jumped out of her seat and could barely sit for the remainder of the conversation. In another session, we were discussing one of her goals, which involved producing 100 interviews on her new TV show. Out of the blue, she shared that she had been marijuana-free for two months. As of our last conversation, it's been more than a year. Even though she's still pursuing her Big Thing, she's already created some amazing outcomes. One could argue that this single accomplishment alone made the pursuit of her Big Thing worthwhile.

This is The Big Thing Effect. When you start moving toward your Big Thing, other things get handled—either they dissolve, or you've accessed a bigger part of yourself that's now able to handle those issues with greater ease.

PETER LIGHT:
FOCUSING ON THE BIG THING ELEVATED HIS
IMMEDIATE CIRCUMSTANCES

Peter was frustrated. The year was 2015, and he'd been stuck in a loop for more than a year. A talented engineer with a strong business acumen, he was a Product Manager at a clean energy startup. He also had a knack for explaining complex technology to clients and potential investors. After being passed over for a long-promised promotion, he tried everything to shift his situation, but nothing seemed to matter. He wondered why he was being passed over. He scheduled meetings with the CEO, but something always came up. He struggled to strengthen his voice and lobby for his ideas. Every day burned away in delay, red tape, and endless to-dos. He was busy, but wasn't having the impact he wanted. More concerning was the growing discontent that left him feeling off-track.

In our early meetings, Peter was intent on making personal changes to become more valuable in his job. With a new baby at home, and the high cost of living in San Francisco, he was determined to gain some ground. To his surprise, I began by asking him about his future.

"But I have real issues to tackle *now*," he insisted.

I challenged Peter to slow down, to explore, and to identify the Big Thing that he ultimately wanted to do. He was drowning in the day-to-day, with no time to devote to this larger question. On a hike overlooking the Pacific, Peter exclaimed, "I want to be a pioneer of clean energy technology!"

I asked what that meant, and we spent the next two hours exploring what he wanted that to look and feel like. He wanted to be a person who inspired meaningful change in clean energy. He desired to be a leader who made clean energy accessible to people all over the world. As Peter articulated his vision, his face lit up and he quickened the pace. I had to hustle to keep up.

Because Peter was willing to enlarge his vision, he allowed his Big Thing to speak to him. It was in there, but he was previously so busy, it didn't have time to come out. Many people would have insisted that they wait a year or for a time when it's more convenient, but there's no convenient time to transform your life. That's a mirage. Your only access to change is *now*. Some tell themselves they'll address this question when they retire. Luckily for Peter, I didn't let him off the hook. Remember, it may take some coaxing, but your Big Thing is in there, and when it comes out, it transforms your life.

Peter started devoting calendar time each week to clarifying the vision of his Big Thing. After he clarified what it looked and felt like, he committed. As Peter spent more and more time seeing his Big Thing, he began to feel excitement and momentum. The more he *saw* it, the more he *felt* it.

Excitement about his Big Thing grew into an obsession, and he was already starting to exude the very qualities of that *future* Peter. In a few months, he was inspired like never before when, seemingly out of the blue, the CEO gave him the long-awaited promotion. Then, something remarkable happened. Headhunters started calling, unsolicited, asking if he would interview. This surprised him because he wasn't looking for a new job. He hadn't even expressed dissatisfaction to his colleagues.

Peter accepted a few of these interviews simply to see what they were offering. One of those was at Google's moonshot innovation company, Google X. They wanted Peter to manage a new wind technology product called Makani. It was an exciting opportunity; not only would he be part of the engineering team, he would also participate in business development and leadership. His innovative ideas would directly contribute to this project's success. Peter accepted the new position.

This new role elevated his visibility, broadened his experience, and expanded his relationships. Now, he had major resources at his fingertips. The organizational red tape was not as tangled, and he was able to affect more change with greater ease. Not only that; over the course of the next year, he significantly increased his income.

Peter's story illustrates that clarifying and committing to your Big Thing can have immediate and positive impact in your life. Rather than being a distraction, it can often be an accelerator. Peter is now CEO and cofounder of Lumen Energy. Their breakthrough software enables commercial building owners to profitably cut carbon. They are currently serving thousands of buildings nationwide.

Getting Comfortable with Discomfort

While your Big Thing will move you into your discomfort zone, there's an antidote—getting comfy in discomfort.

I used to spend a lot of energy trying to dissipate discomfort. It was a major distraction. As I shared earlier in the chapter, I came face-to-face with my acrophobia on Longs Peak, when there was nowhere to go and nothing to distract me. Guard against the temptation to numb yourself and avoid this rich energy of discomfort. It is not to be numbed. Instead, it's meant to be used as fuel. Use the discomfort to transform the fear into doing the thing that scares you. The first step to transform discomfort into fuel is to accept it.

Be careful not to judge the sensation of discomfort. Instead, re-label it as good and necessary. When I experience discomfort now, I say to myself, "Oh wow, this is exciting. I'm feeling discomfort! This is added energy for this task ahead. When I use this as fuel and channel it, good things happen." This reframing helps to properly empower you around the discomfort, and this new interpretation is closer to reality than the old story, "This is bad, it hurts, so it must mean something is off." What happens when you believe that story? You back away from taking action. The consequence is a roller coaster of inconsistency.

Observing Your Feelings vs Judging Them

The second step toward utilizing discomfort is to feel your feelings. Slow down to the speed of life and actually experience what's going on inside. I'm referring to the emotions that cycle beneath the surface as well as the physiological sensations in the body. Yet most of us are so busy, we're actually doing the opposite. We're *thinking* about what we're feeling, but not actually experiencing it. Slowing down to acknowledge what's going on inside is a powerful thing.

WILLIAM:
MOVING THROUGH
MAJOR LEAGUE STRESS

One of my clients, William, owns a major league sports team. Recently, he was in the process of making some big changes that were important for the health of the franchise and its future. There was hate mail, attempts to defame his character, and even death threats. At one point he said, "I don't know if I can do this. People are completely misunderstanding my intentions." In addition, he was second-guessing his decisions and doubting his instincts. To use his words, the stress was, "eating him up."

I had him close his eyes, breathe deeply and feel every sensation in his body. It was challenging for him not to go into a story about the feeling. His mind, like everyone's, wanted to attach meaning to the intense sensations he felt. Yet, the more he let go of his mind and witnessed what he was feeling, the sensation shifted. Within moments, his face softened, and his body relaxed.

Once he actually allowed himself to experience the sensations circulating beneath, he was reconnected with his resilient, wise, and clear self. We didn't psychoanalyze those feelings or even try to reframe them as "good." Each time he mentioned the stress building up, or if I saw him getting uptight, I would interrupt and encourage him to feel and resist nothing. It was as though he was washed clean. His face became flush with color again, and he smiled. After these moments of feeling, he said, "This is the right decision. I have to trust it and not take things so personally."

We often unknowingly run from our intense feelings. Our natural response is to avoid or numb ourselves from this sensation. This avoidance produces a problem all its own, a sensation of separation inside. We feel cut off because we are. On a certain level, our brain says, "I can't do this. This feeling is bad," and then we avoid it. However, if you slow down and breathe, you will realize that the sensation is simply energy. When you allow it and experience it, the energy can move through you, rather than get lodged in your body and generate even more disturbance.

When we slow down and feel our feelings, we actually "come home" within ourselves. This is one of the highest forms of self-acceptance.

If this emotional health is ignored, it will become an obstacle that will make it very difficult to move forward. This practice will help you make proactive choices from a state of clarity rather than reaction. Most of us are waiting for someone else to show up and be totally accepting of what we're feeling and not walk away. We want someone *else* to sit with us in our deepest emotion and be with us. Yet, real change comes when we do it for ourselves.

When you still yourself enough to experience the physiological sensation inside, without judgment, and without letting your mind create a story about what the feeling *means*, you'll be at the doorway to mastering choice. Until you can be still, you don't have choice. Your choices have you.

Be in the Present
Slowing down and being present creates a sense of harmony inside. This feeling of harmony is essential if you want to go all the way with your Big Thing. So far, we've spent ample time discussing the importance of clarifying your Big Thing and creating a vision. Once the vision is clear, remember to shift your focus to the present moment: *One step at a time and everything's fine.* This will increase your power and give you an edge that many are looking for but few know where to find.

Exercise:
The 5-Minute "Feels" Exercise

Take a moment, sit down, and feel what's going on inside of you, right now. How do you feel physically? What do you feel emotionally? Bring your attention to what you're feeling. You might notice, "I'm feeling annoyed, I feel agitated, and there's a tingly sensation in my stomach." If so, then bring your awareness to those sensations one at a time. Allow them. Don't resist. Feel them. Let the sensation be there and experience it fully. Be curious about the sensation, like a detective picking up clues. "Hey, that's sadness. Hmmm, that's an interesting sensation. Ooo, it's warm, and feels tingly in my stomach." Then feel it. Don't wish it away or go into thinking about it. Don't make up stories about it.

Now, breathe directly into the part of your body where you feel that sensation. Feel, breathe, accept, observe. That's it. Doing this will give you back your freedom. The more you do this, the more you remove the need for distraction because most of your distracting behavior comes from not experiencing your feelings. This is why meditation is so powerful, yet challenging. Doing it requires you to simply sit with what you're feeling and do nothing with it. Just breathe and allow it to be there.

Don't take my word for it. Try it. Then notice how you feel. If you're like me, the feeling often quickly dissipates. You'll also begin to experience a sense of centeredness and quiet strength.

CHAPTER 6

Shift Your Way of Being

MY NEED TO BE "NICE"
NEARLY KILLED US

November 10, 2010 • Training Climb • James Peak, Colorado

Six months into our training, our seven-man team spent the night above timberline during a winter training climb on James Peak in central Colorado. The dawn broke clear and blue. In three hours, we reached the summit, well ahead of schedule. We dawdled, shot pictures, re-sorted our packs, and took in the view.

Feeling spent and tired, I really wanted to get back down, but didn't want to be the party pooper. I had the distinct sense that if we didn't leave now, something bad would happen. Wind was picking up, and I was feeling sweaty and chilled. I wanted to say, "Hey guys, let's get off this summit before the weather changes," but I hesitated. I thought to myself, *You don't have enough experience, and they'll think you're being bossy,* so I deferred. Instead of getting off the mountain, we passed around a thermos of coffee.

The next gust knocked me off my feet. Suddenly, we were blinded by a whiteout driven by sixty mile-per-hour winds at 13,301 feet. Scrambling to descend, three of us somehow became separated from the rest. No tracks. No trace. Only snow blowing sideways.

We fumbled down the slope, unaware that we were skirting the edge of a 1,000-foot cornice, an overhanging mass of ice that often forms at the edge of a mountain's precipice. After about an hour, as the wind relented, we could finally see that this was not the same route we came up. We were lost on the wrong side of the mountain. We had a cellphone but couldn't reach the rest of the team. A 911 operator connected us to Search and Rescue. They were emphatic: "Do not take another step down the mountain or you will fall off the cornice. You have no choice but to climb back up to the summit and then come down the other side."

Seven hours later we collapsed in camp, exhausted and lucky to be alive.

Who Are You Being?

There is what you *do*, there is what you *have*, and there is who you *be*. The last one, who you're *being*, is often overlooked. Your way of being is the unique way you show up in the world.

This training climb exposed a flaw in the way I'd been showing up in the world. It revealed my way of being, namely, being "nice." And it nearly killed us. Avoiding my instincts, discounting my perspective, and not speaking up was everywhere in my life but I hadn't previously seen it, until now. I couldn't continue this way of being and realize my Big Thing.

That experience proved that ignoring my instincts could be fatal. It also illustrated how a small story like, "My team won't like me if I speak up," can have serious consequences. Up to that moment, I was more interested in being liked than being a leader. This was a humbling thing to admit. I named this old way of being "Needy Man."

"Needy Man" needed everyone to like him. He needed to feel appreciated. He needed others' approval to bolster his confidence. He was also more focused on others' opinions of himself than he was in serving others.

This guy, who needed to please everyone and who ignored his instincts, was not going to get me to my Big Thing. Most importantly, he was out of alignment with my Essential Self, who I *really* was.

Driving home from James Peak, I resolved to transform

"Needy Man" into someone empowered. As I drove along the Interstate, a memory came rushing in that reminding me how I had transformed my way of being a decade earlier.

HOW LOW CAN YOU GO?
SHIFTING WHO I NEEDED TO BE
CREATED A BREAKTHROUGH

In 1999, I felt invincible. My Big Thing—"Hosting that show on that stage"—led me to become a working actor in Hollywood. The Nickelodeon gig at Universal Studios led to hosting another Nickelodeon production, a traveling game show called, "Nickelodeon Game Lab." With these two jobs, I had the freedom to audition for commercial work and larger roles in film and TV. By 2000, I was landing commercials frequently. At one point, I had six of them running at the same time, and two were national network spots, the holy grail of commercials. This meant that they were airing everywhere in America in prime time. I'd get calls from family and friends at all hours saying, "Hey, I saw you on TV!" In fact, perhaps the greatest feather in my cap (in my own mind) came when my Busch Light commercial aired during the World Series. I tried to save all the voicemails but the tape in the answering machine ran out.

Then disaster struck.

In May of 2000, two unions, the Screen Actors Guild, and the American Federation of Television & Radio Artists, went on strike. It completely shut down the commercial acting industry in Hollywood. There were offers on the side, but if I crossed the picket lines I could be blackballed. It was the longest work stoppage in Hollywood history, lasting six months.

Like everyone else in LA, I kept thinking, "this will end soon," so I continued living like nothing had changed. After all, I was a working actor. I started living on credit cards. Things eventually got so bad that I had to take a day job, selling used cars at a Honda dealership in Santa Monica.

When the strike finally ended, residuals had stopped

coming in, and I had lost momentum. Over the next year, fewer commercials were being shot, everyone was in the same boat, and the business was more competitive than ever. I didn't have a single audition for almost a year. There was no work to be had. I was stuck selling cars.

With the mounting financial stress, I was more anxious than ever. I was judging myself as a loser who deserved punishment. This pulled my normal energetic demeanor into a dark depression. I couldn't see what to do to pull myself out of this hole. I was so focused on what I needed to *do* that I overlooked the more important aspect: who I needed to *be*.

Then, sitting at the dingy desk under the fluorescent glare of the Honda showroom, inspiration struck. While I couldn't see what I was doing in the future, I could imagine who I was *being*. I could see the *future me*. I could see how I was showing up, how I operated. (You could also say that this was who I wanted to be in the future.)

That future me was playful and generous. He took excellent care of himself. Bold and courageous, he used intuition and emotional sensitivity to tune in and help people. He was playful and used humor in his everyday interactions. He also challenged others to go for their dreams and helped them with his counsel. He was caring and generous and did what he believed was right, even if it went against popular opinion. This was not how I'd been showing up. While I didn't know what steps I needed to take to get back on track with my acting career, I knew I wanted to be *that* guy *at the dealership*, but I didn't think I could. I had a preconception of what a used car salesman was. I thought I needed to get a different job before I could be caring, conscious, and confident.

I had an epiphany! I was lost because I was obsessed with knowing what I needed to *do*. What was so depressing was not what I was *doing*. It was who I was *being*. I was judging the job and not bringing my whole self to it. I was showing up as what I thought a "used car salesman" *should* be, instead of being my authentic self, who just *happened* to be selling cars. I thought I had to suppress the real me and suffer through this. Suppressing the real you causes suffering, and it wasn't the dealership's fault, or the car business. It was me. It was who I was *being*.

The task was not to choose which direction to go. My opportunity was to shift who I was being and bring forward this (future) version of myself *now*. If I couldn't be that version of Jeff Patterson now, what made me think I could be him in the future? What was I waiting for?

I wrote that version down on paper. Then each day I imagined how he would show up and how he would approach the day. This was like a fun improvisation where I role-played this future me. I would often write this out in my journal, playing out the exciting ways I would operate as him in the day ahead. Then, after my morning writing I would go out and do my best to operate *as him*.

What I learned was that it wasn't enough to simply *act* like him. I needed to *view the world* as he did. I began to imagine how *he* thought and what *he* believed (which was very unlike how I was thinking and believing at that time). Through my imagination, I observed the things he focused on. I also noticed the qualities that he was exuding. This gave me a new inner roadmap and supported *being* him.

What happened in the following months shocked everyone. I had more fun than ever. This shift toward showing up as the future Jeff produced a dramatic change in my experience.

I started *being* more playful. I used my intuition and started operating like my Future Self. I became more focused on serving customers than I was in their opinions about me as a car salesman. I also stopped judging myself. This led to me to doing goofy impersonations of all the people I worked with. It wasn't long before Friday nights at the dealership became Standup Night where I would do impersonations on demand.

Because I was being the "me" I wanted to be, I felt fulfilled. I stopped searching for the ideal circumstance, the perfect job, and started *being* the ideal *me* in the exact circumstances I was in. I had also moved up to #1 in sales. I was having so much fun that I didn't want to leave. In less than six months, I landed a hosting gig for E! Entertainment that lifted me out of the dealership and put me back on track toward my Hollywood Big Thing.

We Create from the Level of Being

When people attempt to perform at a higher level, they often merely adjust their behavior. *If I do things differently, that should produce a different result.* However, to create a true breakthrough that sticks, you must go deeper to the level of being. By shifting your focus, thinking, and qualities of being, you will naturally spark new actions that were previously invisible. This is creating from being, rather than simply pushing harder.

This goes beyond the Law of Attraction, which is about being aligned with the qualities you want. We're taking it a vital step further. By being the "you" that you must be in order to realize your Big Thing, you're not only a vibrational match, but you also *act* in new and different ways that cause new and different results. This action-oriented element is what makes this doubly effective.

What's a vibrational match? Think of the times when you're excited or filled with joy. You feel energetic, motivated, and positive. Consequently, your energetic "state" rises. As a result, the other things that emit a similar vibration of energy will draw to you and align around you. (Remember the experiment in school with the iron filings and the magnet? It's like that.) However, the opposite happens as well. When you feel depressed, with low energy, other low energy people, situations, and objects will be drawn to you. Like attracts like. Birds of a feather.

What you create in life is directly related to how you *see* life and, most importantly, how you see *yourself*. Are you seeing yourself as you *are*, or as you *fear* yourself to be?

NO MORE
"MR. NICE GUY"
November 20, 2010 • Aconcagua training continues

A week after the near-disaster on James Peak, I had the opportunity to meet with the CEO of one of the top sporting apparel companies in the world. He and his wife were interested in coaching, and we met to explore if we were a good fit.

We had a deep, inspiring conversation about what they wanted to create and what might be in the way. The meeting ended with them committing to a year of coaching. I should have felt great, but, as I drove home, a feeling of remorse washed over me. Pulling the car over, I searched for anything that would explain this.

I decided to call Stephen. From the perspective of a coach, he'd be able to help examine the situation in a way that I couldn't on my own. Through our conversation about that meeting, I saw that I had intuitively picked up things that I didn't share in the moment. I realized that I didn't speak up because I doubted my instincts and feared what might happen if I actually shared them.

This was out of alignment with the kind of coach I was committed to being. But because I revered this CEO, I started *being* careful and cautious. I wanted him to like me. More importantly, I feared that he wouldn't hire me if I shared what I was seeing. So, I withheld what I saw to please him and in hopes of getting his business.

This was embarrassing. My need to be liked and that old habit of pleasing to get approval had taken over again. *Ughhh!* I had reverted back into "Needy Man."

Stephen asked, "Who do you want to be instead?"

"I want to be an impactful leader, who helps people create incredible results in their lives and businesses. I want to inspire clients to extraordinary heights and to become who they're destined to be."

Stephen blurted, "Who you're describing isn't Needy Man, it's *Miracle Man*! He helps clients create miracles."

At first, I cringed. "Miracle Man" sounded … dorkey … religious … and arrogant. I wasn't sure which was worse, but I caught the spirit of what he was saying. From this new mindset of "Miracle Man," on the side of the road, I called back the CEO.

"Andy, I want to clean something up with you. In our conversation today, I wasn't totally open with you about all of my observations. I saw more than I shared. After I left, I felt a heavy feeling for not having had the courage to be fully authentic."

"Jeff, I think you're being hard on yourself. I thought the conversation was powerful and very helpful. There's nothing to clean up."

"I hear you," I continued, "but I'm committed to being absolutely authentic with clients and deeply serving them. Even though you said you want to work together, it's important to clean this up and be in integrity with myself. Can we meet one more time, at no charge to you? I'd like to put everything on the table, and, once I have, if you're still clear that you'd like to work together, then let's move forward."

He agreed, and the three of us met again. The result was an even more inspired conversation in which we discussed all the insights and observations that had been withheld in the first meeting. This created a deeper level of trust and transparency, and we went on to work together for four years.

Back at home, I wrote down a description of who Miracle Man was, the qualities he embodied, how he thought, what made him tick, what he focused on, and how he operated in the world.

Miracle Man was courageous. He was committed to being authentic. He believed his instincts made a difference to his clients and shared them. Miracle Man would never ignore his intuition, avoid uncomfortable conversations, or worry about what others thought about him.

I called it the "Miracle Man Manifesto." I began to read it daily. Soon I began to evoke his qualities. I started taking action from the perspective of Miracle Man. I created a new game called, "What would Miracle Man do?" (WWMMD). This was not, "fake it 'til you make it." It was, "be it 'til you see it." I wasn't simply acting like him... I was committed to *being* him.

If you really want to create transformation, it's not enough to simply change your behavior at the external level. You have to go beneath, to the internal level, and shift your way of being. Otherwise, those behaviors will not be sustainable. You will default back into your old conditioning.

And, once you begin to operate from your new way of being, know that you will slip back from time to time. That's not a problem. It's part of the process.

Every time I'd exhibit Needy Man behavior, I'd acknowledge it: "There goes Needy Man." I was learning to bring awareness to something that was previously unconscious. If I could see where I was being unlike who I wanted to be, I could choose to be something else.

The more I took action from the new perspective of Miracle Man, the more his characteristics would show up. I felt this shift immediately, but it took some time to turn into a habit. With every action, I began to feel more and more like him. It was not without challenges, but I was seeing my life through a different lens, and I could feel things shifting.

As a result, I was relating differently to everyone in my life, especially clients. I acted more assertively on my instincts. I spoke up more, said things that needed to be said, and didn't hold back in the ways Needy Man had previously.

One of the most significant aspects of this profound change was the evidence of my inner shift in the outer world. Not only were clients generating substantially bigger results, but there were several instances when clients literally used the words "miracle" and "miraculous" to describe their progress.

Upgrade Your Conditioned Self

Consider this question: Who do you need to *be* to realize your Big Thing?

Shifting your way of being to match the outcome you

desire, instantly connects you to the qualities within that you need to reach it.

As we discussed in Chapter 2, there are two aspects of yourself that inform your way of being: your Essential Self and your Conditioned Self. Again, your Essential Self is your *true* self, or soul. Your Conditioned Self is your *created* self. The self you learned to be, the self you were conditioned to be, by family, friends, society. You can systematically alter your way of being on the Conditioned Self level.

Your Conditioned Self determines how much of your Essential Self can shine through. Because of this, The Conditioned Self is the greatest impactor of your inner experience as well as your outer results.

There are four elements that determine your Conditioned Self:

1. **Your focus**—Where you consistently place your attention. What you focus on expands and grows.
2. **Your qualities**—The main qualities of being that you're choosing to cultivate and embody.
3. **Your thinking**—Your beliefs about yourself (self-identity), others, the world around you.
4. **Your habits**—The behaviors you engage in regularly.

To upgrade your Conditioned Self, you want to make sure that your focus, qualities, thinking, and habits are all aligned with your Big Thing. A great way to do this is to ask this simple question: *Who do I need to be to realize my Big Thing?*

Then go down the list of the four elements, and answer these questions.

- What would you have to focus on consistently?
- What one to three qualities would you have to embody?
- What one to three thoughts would you need to think consistently in order to reach your Big Thing?
- Finally, what habits would you have to demonstrate consistently to reach your Big Thing?

Answering these questions will give you a powerful blueprint for upgrading your Conditioned Self and elevating your way of being.

Once you answer those questions and start to shift your focus, cultivate certain qualities, think new thoughts about yourself, and engage in the new habits, you'll start to be the version of yourself that you need to be to create what you want to achieve. I'm challenging you to commit to operating *from* this new identity. Acting from this new perspective will propel you toward your Big Thing. This technology is especially effective with teams.

THE SIOUX FALLS STAMPEDE: BEING A CHAMPION PRECEDES WINNING A CHAMPIONSHIP

In 2012, when Bob Naegele and his partners purchased the Sioux Falls Stampede hockey club, they were a perennial underachieving team in the United States Hockey League. Fan attendance was waning. Within eighteen months, Bob and his partners changed head coaches and began shifting the culture of the organization on both the business and the hockey side. It was during this time that Bob called to see how I might be able to help. It was an exciting opportunity.

A few days later, I stood in the locker room before this group of seventeen to twenty-year-olds. Most had Division I college scholarships already secure. I asked them to define their Big Thing for the upcoming season. The players and coaches unanimously agreed it was to win the Clark Cup, the USHL's version of the NHL Stanley Cup.

The next question silenced the room: "Who do you need to be in order to win the championship?"

We had a deep conversation about the distinction between being a champion versus winning a championship.

I told the team, "You can't just go for a championship. That's only the outcome. What happens when you seem to be off track? How do you know how to get back on the road to the top? You may have the X's and O's, the systems and strategies to lead you, but that's not enough. Champions are forged from the inside. What leads you to the top is not only the action you take on the ice, but the way of being you embody along the way. You don't *become* a champion by winning a championship. You win a championship by *being* a champion."

I challenged each of them to describe how they would have to think, what they would have to consistently focus on, and how they would have to show up. Together, we explored the unique qualities they would have to embody, as individuals, and as a team, in order to win the Clark Cup.

I went to the whiteboard and wrote, "Who do you need to be?"

"Relentless," one player shouted.

Another yelled, "Do what's right for the team, not just what's right for me."

I asked, "What does that mean?"

"Well, I'd have to be willing to switch positions if Coach wanted me to. I'd have to give it everything I've got; whether we're ahead or behind doesn't matter."

"I'd have to be more disciplined in the off-season," said another.

They knew. They could see the shifts that needed to happen. This was not an external game plan to give them. It was a hidden blueprint that I was helping them unlock.

We went farther to identify what they would have to focus on consistently. We explored the mindset they would have to embody in order to realize their goal. After leading them to identify their new way of being, I challenged them with a question.

"Are you willing to go out and be that team? Not pretend to be, but to actually *be* that team. To think those thoughts, focus on those elements and cultivate those qualities. Are you willing to operate from this perspective while playing full out toward the Cup?"

Heads nodded, and players called out "yes."

Then I asked, "Do you need *anything* in order to start showing up in this new way?"

"No!"

"Do you need one more win in order to be more selfless?"

"No!"

"Do you need more spectators in the stands to be more disciplined in your training?"

"No!"

"Do you need more talent, or more skill, or more experience in order to embody the quality of being relentless?"

"No!"

Then someone added, "The talent and skills we need will grow from this new way of being."

Heads nodded, and shouts of "Yes!" exploded like popcorn.

Something had clicked in the collective mind of this team.

"This is what it means to *be* a champion, and you don't need one thing to start operating from this stance. Other teams are *waiting* to win a championship. But not you. You can be that now. Stop waiting and hoping things will change. Stop looking for outside validation. Decide today. Make the decision, right now, that this is who you are, and deliver this way of being, starting now. Will you do it?"

"Yeah!!!" The place went nuts.

That night, the Stampede played a home game and pummeled their opponents. They went on to finish in the top three in their division, advancing to the playoffs, something they hadn't done in three years. They lost in the semi-finals, but returned the following season to become league champions, winning the esteemed Clark Cup.

To this day, the Stampede remains a top performer on and off the ice, setting new league attendance records four years in a row.

The Myth of "I'm just that way"

Surely, you've heard someone say something along the lines of, "I always wanted to do theater, but I'm terribly afraid of standing in front of audiences." This person could shut down their dream because of the perception of *who they are,* or they could *transform* their perception of themself to align with their dream. There are those who shrink their Big Thing to fit their personality, and there are those who allow the expansiveness of their Big Thing to transform their personality. A personality, much like the Conditioned Self, is "a characteristic way of thinking, feeling, and behaving." (Britannica.com)

Many people have unconsciously thwarted an inspired life because they've decided what they want is out of alignment with who they are. They falsely believe they're stuck in a fixed personality, but personalities are malleable. Identities can be rewritten as fast as a Hollywood sitcom. Change who you're *being* so that it aligns with your Big Thing, rather than shrinking down your Big Thing to squeeze into your current way of operating.

DAYNAMITE:
A NEW YOU, A NEW OUTCOME

A few years ago, Dayna came to me saying she was stuck. After ten years in the competitive world of real estate, she thought she might need to change careers. Within minutes, I could see Dayna was bright, intelligent, and savvy. She was charismatic, a delight to be around. Yet she was struggling in her business.

She was sick and tired of having so much potential but not converting it successfully. Her Big Thing? To generate $10 million in her business that year. To set some context, $10 million in sales was more than what she'd sold in her previous decade, combined.

I helped her look honestly at how she'd been showing up in her business, and where it wasn't working. With an open heart, she confessed to being highly focused on what clients thought of her and only lightly focused on the results they wanted to achieve. Because of that, she second-guessed herself and hesitated, which delayed her follow-through. This, in turn, impacted her business, as well as clients' confidence in her.

Because of this dynamic, she was also not consistently asking tough questions or asking for the sale. She began to see the reason she was struggling. She saw the connection between who she was *being* and the shortfall in results.

It takes vulnerability and self-honesty to look at these issues. Dayna owned all of it.

Now that we had a clear look at how she was previously showing up, we explored who she would have to *be* to create her Big Thing.

"I'd have to be courageous as well as vulnerable to ask the direct questions I've been afraid to ask. I'd have to focus more on my clients' results than on my fear of failing. I'd have to take action immediately, rather than avoiding the things that might be uncomfortable." She continued, "I'd have to choose to believe that I have what it takes."

I said, "Let's give that person you described a name." Together we came up with "Daynamite."

She adopted a new story. There was the *old* Dayna, who was hesitant, scattered, and lacked follow-through, and the *new* Dayna*mite* who is courageous, direct, and proactive. Daynamite asked the tough questions. Daynamite followed through. Daynamite asked for the sale.

I high-fived her, "Your mission, should you choose to accept it, is to unleash Daynamite in your life *right now* as you play full out toward your Big Thing. I want you to leave the office and *be* her. Deliver that way of being right where you are. You will not respond as Dayna. You will respond as Daynamite."

Dayna started showing up as Daynamite, yet the old voices were still clamoring: "My clients won't appreciate this change. Who do I think I am anyway? I'm still the old fear-filled me. This is uncomfortable. It must not be working. I'm going to fail!"

The resistance didn't dissipate immediately. This was scary at first, but I assured her that this is a very normal and important part of the process.

The difference now was that she was committed to addressing the voices as Daynamite. She listened, wrote them down, and challenged them. Step-by-step, day-by-day, she continued operating as Daynamite. She was vulnerable by acknowledging when she needed help. She took great care of herself by asking for the necessary support on multiple fronts. She also engaged in excellent and consistent self-care, which was now a habit of Daynamite.

She had a new mindset, a fresh identity, and a different way of operating. She was *being* Daynamite even before she saw any outer results physically manifest. This inner shift prompted new actions and reactions. People noticed the change. She began to attract a whole new clientele, and colleagues wanted to collaborate. It transformed her business and her life.

This new way of being impacted other areas as well, such as her relationships. After being single for a long time, she started a relationship with a man she described as her soul mate. They're now happily married with a growing blended family. She says she never would have met him without becoming Daynamite.

Within a year, she closed $15 million in commissionable sales. And, so far this year, she's closed $96 Million and she's only half way through the year.

Exercise:
Creating Your New Way of Being

The following 8-step exercise will walk you through who you need to be in order to realize your Big Thing.

Step 1: Imagine the Future You

Imagine time traveling into the future and meeting the "you" who has already created your Big Thing. We're hopping in the time machine and visiting your Future Self to observe. By watching and learning about how they think, what they focus on, the qualities they exude, the lengths they're willing to go, we can see how they're uniquely different from how you've been operating up 'til now.

Through this creative process, we're going to bring that person back to your current digs, unleash them in your life, and let *them* lead the way. How is this possible? The future you lies dormant, deep in your unconscious. You can call forward those qualities, attributes, and strengths from the depths.

Step 2: Describe Your New Way of Being
- What must you focus on consistently? ("I must focus on what I'm doing well.")
- What three attributes of being must you embody? (Courage, Persistence, Self-Trust, etc.)
- What three beliefs must you hold? ("I can do this." "I was born to do this," "I choose to do this," etc.)
- What's one *new* habit you must build?
- What's one *old* habit you must break?
- What does the future you *always* do?
- What does the future you *never* do?
- How far is this version of you willing to go?
- What's *uncommon* about your Future Self that is distinct from who you've *been* being up 'til now?

After answering these questions, notice what stands out. Are there any repeating ideas? Next, take your responses to those questions and write a *New You Manifesto* in a separate document. Take each of your responses from above and turn them into "I am" statements. So, for example, here is a portion of the manifesto I came up with after the James Peak climb:

The New You Manifesto: *"I am Miracle Man. I am courageous. My experience and presence help people create miracles in their lives and businesses. I'm deeply intuitive and trust my instincts. I take ample time every day to cultivate these gifts. I'm committed. When I say I will do something, it is done. I stop at nothing to deliver on my word. I care too much about people to care what they think of me."*

Step 3. List Your Old Way vs. New Way of Being

In addition to a manifesto, some people find it very helpful to make a chart with two columns, one listing their old way of being and the other, their new way. This really simplifies the distinction and helps you to know, at any moment, which way of being you're operating from. This is demonstrated in the graph on the next page (137).

Step 4. Name Your Old and Your New Way of Being

Give the old you a name, like "Needy Man," and then give the new you a name as well (like "Miracle Man," or "Daynamite.")

Step 5. Read Your Manifesto Daily

For the next two weeks, carry your manifesto with you everywhere and read it out loud *at least* ten times a day, the more often the better. It's not enough to think about it. You have to speak it out loud. Give it tons of attention. We become what we obsess about. Make this an obsession!

Step 6. Take Action from Your New Way of Being

Now, start living from this new perspective. Take action that's aligned with these beliefs, focus, and qualities. Start cultivating these qualities of being in your life. Begin thinking these new thoughts and living in alignment with all of it to your very best.

To begin with, *take one small action* that's aligned with the New You. Ask yourself, "What's one tiny step I could take, *right now,* that's aligned with this new story?" Intuitively, you'll *know* the answer (go for a walk, review my vision, return Shelly's call…). Just do that.

Keep it tiny. It's a phone call. It's a note to yourself. It seems miniscule. As Neil Armstrong said, "That's one small step…."

Step 7. Course Correct When You Fall Back

It's normal to have your old way of being step back into the picture. When you catch yourself operating out of the old way, pause and *thank* it for showing up. Each occurrence is a gift that

NEEDY MAN

3 QUALITIES:
1. SELF-DOUBT
2. SELF-JUDGMENT – Constant criticism and expectation of perfection.
3. PLEASING – Obsessing over what others think of him to the point of not knowing what he truly wants and feels.

3 BELIEFS:
1. "I'm not ready."
2. "Others are better qualified than me."
3. "I am not enough."

FOCUS:
Focused more on what others think of him than on what he thinks of himself. Focused more on getting than on what he's giving (serving.) Focused in his fearful thoughts.

HABIT:
Unconsciously eating sugar to avoid feelings of insecurity.

ALWAYS:
He always assumed bad things were about to happen. He always thought others had something he didn't have.

NEVER:
Needy Man would never speak his truth if he feared it might upset someone.

UNCOMMON:
• What was uncommon about Needy Man was that he analyzed every feeling and usually created a negative story about the feeling.
• He was hesitant, careful, and quiet. He was afraid of making a mistake or upsetting someone. He didn't share himself fully.

MIRACLE MAN

3 QUALITIES:
1. COURAGE – Stay committed even if scared.
2. SELF-ACCEPTANCE – Appreciation of what's good.
3. COMMITMENT – "All in" on this endeavor and consistently being the me I want to be and not let the fear of failure have me BE something else.

3 BELIEFS:
1. "I make a difference."
2. "Self-care accelerates my ability to serve others."
3. "My gift, and sharing it, is a gift in the world."

FOCUS:
He focuses more on what he wants to create than what he's afraid could happen. He focuses more on serving others than on their opinions.

HABIT:
Consistent habit of doing personal work and self-care that he knows lifts him up.

ALWAYS:
Miracle Man always honors his word. He follows through on his promises. If he doesn't, he quickly acknowledges it and cleans it up.

NEVER:
Miracle Man never ignores his intuition.

UNCOMMON:
• He is uncommonly committed to cultivating his gifts, especially his intuition.
• He's bold and goes to great lengths to serve those in his care. He shares what he sees will benefit others, even if it ruffles feathers. He's a leader not a pleaser and he does it with great passion, love, and creativity.

137

helps you redirect your attention. Respond by affirming the New You. Shift your attention to the statements in your New You Manifesto and speak them *aloud*, as if the words you're speaking are planting seeds into the soil of your life. With each repetition, they grow and strengthen. Every time you catch yourself acting out of the *old* story, speak the new story, *out loud*. Then take a small action. When Needy Man would creep in and take the wheel at times, I'd ask myself, "WWMMD?"

As you move forward, begin to notice the many ways you're operating in alignment with the New You Manifesto. Identify any small evidence that you're demonstrating this new way of being.

Then take it a step further. When you act *out* of alignment with your new way of being, go back and clean it up.

Using my example, call back the CEO and acknowledge that you chickened out. You might confess that you were afraid of what they would think. Acknowledge that you were more concerned with their opinion than serving the project. You might say something like, "That was the *old* me, and I wasn't being real with you. I apologize for that. What can I do to clean that up?" By cleaning it up, you'll put your consciousness on notice that there are consequences for not being who you are committed to. This adds healthy leverage which accelerates the integration.

Step 8. Always Be Celebrating

Each time you take action, no matter how small, pat yourself on the back with acknowledgment. In fact, celebrate each time you notice any part of this *new* you showing up in your thoughts, feelings, or behavior. The more action you take and acknowledge, the deeper it sticks. In time, this will become effortless.

This doesn't happen overnight. It happens one thought, one action, one shift of focus at a time. In order to have these new subtle changes take hold, it's really important to acknowledge even the *smallest* increment of progress.

To reinforce my new way of being, I began using a line that

I borrowed from *Glengarry Glen Ross*. In the film, Alec Baldwin's character makes up a catchphrase to coach his team of salesmen: "ABC … Always be closing." I gave it my own twist and started saying to myself, "ABC … Always be celebrating." The more you celebrate each micro step forward in this new way of living, the more it comes alive in you. You may feel silly appreciating yourself so fervently and consistently, but doing so acts like Miracle Grow on your transformation.

CHAPTER 7

Turn Obstacles into Opportunities

ALTITUDE ADJUSTMENT

January 18, 2011
Expedition Prep • Mendoza, Argentina • 2,523 feet

After nine months of intense training, the time had finally come to take all our prep and put it on Mt. Aconcagua. We arrived in Mendoza, Argentina after two days of travel. While our excitement level was high, we were exhausted from unexpected delays and cancelled flights. The airlines were on strike, and, at one point, we were concerned we might not even make it to Argentina. That night, our team of seven went to a small restaurant for dinner to meet our three guides. We discussed the permits we needed to purchase the next day and the gear that we still needed to acquire. Augusto, one of our guides who had recently returned from climbing Everest, warned us not to overpack. He said, "Ounces equal pounds, and pounds equal pain."

The dinner was decadent. We drank Malbec and feasted on steaks thick as a dictionary. It was difficult to relax and enjoy our meal because all I could think about was the mountain. It was like a ghost hiding in the night, and I worried that if I enjoyed myself too much, I might not be ready to handle what it might deliver.

After two days of last-minute gear prep and securing permits, we shuttled 250 miles west to the small village of Los Penitentes, and by village, I mean "hotel," as this was the only sign of life within 50 miles. This was a popular ski resort in winter. Now, in summer, it was more like a western ghost town, with the exception of the ten rooms in the hotel, and a small kitchen that prepared meals daily for climbers staging expeditions. We would spend the night so we could start early the next morning.

As we shuffled into the cramped lobby, another team of six climbers was waiting for their shuttle back to Mendoza. They spoke English with thick Swedish accents. They were hoarse and disoriented, but we could make out that they had retreated from the mountain on their third day. I was trying to focus on check-in, but it was hard not to hear their rant about how terrible the trip had been. There was talk of diarrhea and something about one of them having to be helicoptered out due to altitude sickness.

One man with a pale and swollen face came right up to me. He looked like a prize fighter who had just lost a long bout. "This place is dangerous. This was a big mistake. You shouldn't be here." This was not the welcome I'd expected.

My room had the same olive carpet as my grandparent's house in the Midwest, with the added musty smell of dogs and cigars. Judging by the Zenith TV on the pedestal in the corner, the room had been frozen in time in 1967. I slapped the twin bed with my palm and watched dust billow into the sliver of sunlight that squeezed through the small window. I decided to sleep on top of the comforter for fear of what might be crawling beneath. Staring at the ceiling for hours, I tried to push the Swedish climber's face out of my mind.

Day 1
January 20, 2011 • Trailhead to Mt. Aconcagua
Horcones, Argentina • 9,678 feet

We rose early, piled into two vans, and made our way to the trailhead of Aconcagua. Like kids going to camp, we couldn't wipe the smiles off our faces. This was really happening!

The fifteen-minute ride was bumpy. We unpacked at the trailhead and I double checked to ensure all was in order. My pack bulged with sixty pounds of equipment, including a two-man tent, my personal gear, and several pans for melting snow for drinking water and cooking.

The wind kicked up a cloud of red dust and threw it in my face. My stomach was grinding. We gathered in a circle as our lead guide, Mike Bradley, shared a few words to inspire us. "Guys, twenty years from now, you'll forget the many details it took to get here. But I guarantee, you'll always remember these next few weeks on this mountain."

We hiked forty miles over the next three days, reaching basecamp on a glacier at 14,500 feet. Our orange-and-grey tents were surrounded by rock and ice on all sides, with the summit looming like an icy monster. On day four, I bent over to re-tie the tent rigging and felt a blunt throb in my head. I staggered upright, wondering, "Who whacked me with a rock?" It was as if there was a vice tightening on the back of my head and screws being drilled into my eye sockets.

My next thought was, "Oh no… cerebral edema." This is a serious swelling of the brain caused by high altitude. It's claimed the lives of many climbers.

I checked in with the basecamp doctor. Pulse, blood pressure, and oxygenation were relatively normal, so he cleared me to continue. I spoke with Mike and other members of our team. We decided to take an extra day to acclimate, then carry on while keeping a close watch. A storm of self-pity was brewing, and my focus was starting to slide toward my worst fears. This sensation was not new. It was how I operated back home when met with new challenges. After our rest day, we continued up the mountain.

Each day, the pain intensified. Each movement made me nauseous, and my skull throbbed like a migraine times twenty. I was miserable and could not shake it. I was also climbing much slower than the team. I could feel their frustration. I thought, *Maybe I should do everyone a favor and turn around.*

I knew there would be challenges, but this was not at all what I expected. Nothing prepared me for this.

"A thought is only dangerous if you believe it."

There was the agony of the altitude sickness, but there was also another pain that I started to sense. It was an even deeper discomfort. It was a feeling that I didn't *belong* here, an over-all sense that I was not a good person and didn't deserve to succeed. I didn't consciously believe that, yet that's what I was thinking way down inside. It became obvious that this was not a feeling, but a judgment. Many of them.

I began examining my thinking even more. I noticed thoughts like, *Why can't I be more like Greg, who is so upbeat? He has jokes and a kind word at every ridge. Dennis is leading the pack every day and he's 67. What's* my *problem? Vince and Troy are so helpful and kind. What's wrong with me? I don't deserve to be here. I'm such a loser.*

As these thoughts cycled in my mind, there was a heavy, dark feeling in my stomach. It felt like I was about to vomit.

Augusto's warning, "Ounces equal pounds, and pounds equal pain," rang in my mind. I didn't need to jettison extra gear, but I did need to release the unhealthy thoughts weighing me down. The pain was really unpleasant, but what was even more debilitating were the thoughts *about* the pain. *See! You're not ready!! This isn't meant for you!! Who do you think you are? This is a big mistake. You're not going to make it!*

This was a familiar experience. It was how I had met opposition in the past, but I hadn't seen it so clearly before. The mountain acted as a magnifier. It showed me what wasn't working and heightened it. As awful as the feelings were, having them occur on the mountain helped me to both get my arms around them and then let them go. In this way, the challenge was actually presenting me with a gift. Rather than a problem to overcome, this was an opportunity to face challenge in a new way.

Just because I *think* it, doesn't mean it's *true*. I considered, "This *should* be happening. I *should* be feeling this. These are natural responses to altitude, and are the byproduct of actually climbing higher. My body is acclimatizing and adjusting to the new altitude. The headache is part of the journey." Just considering this thought made me feel lighter.

I could see where I was putting suffering on top of the pain. I was then able to experience the pain without the story about it. I decided that if I was going to make up a story, I was going to create an empowering one. I chose to see the altitude sickness as a gift. This new story didn't relieve the pain, but it did remove the suffering, and I felt better.

Your Big Thing Will Reveal What's Holding You Back

As you move toward your Big Thing, anything that's been in the way of stepping into a larger expression of yourself will come to the surface. You might even be unaware of these blocks. Many avoid committing to their Big Thing because of the discomfort that these blocks trigger. These should not be thought of as roadblocks, but rather as *building blocks*. When you face them and accept the gift, you can use them for new insight, direction, and power.

We all face roadblocks in life. The external ones, like being fired from a job, or a colleague undermining you at the office, are often easy to overcome. Like rush hour traffic, they slow you down, but don't prevent you from arriving at your destination. Internal roadblocks, like a lack of commitment, limiting beliefs, or unhealthy patterns, are significantly more dangerous. These must be released so you can realize the fulfillment you desire.

As soon as you commit to your Big Thing, the blocks will start to reveal themselves. This is good. It's essential. It's like a splinter that must work to the surface to get tweezers on it. Often, we're not even aware of the splinter until it comes to the surface. Then it becomes irritating, uncomfortable. Yet, if you slow down and understand it's trying to help, you can release both the discomfort and the block.

AMPCOIL:
COMMITTING TO THEIR BIG THING
HELPED THEM SEE THE BLOCK

In February of 2018, the founders and executive team from Ampcoil, an up-and-coming tech company, flew to Aspen to work with me for two days. During our retreat, I challenged them to declare their Big Thing. Up to this point, the company had been successful, even inspiring, because of their humanitarian intentions. One of their products had been effective in reducing the side effects of Lyme disease and other autoimmune disorders. After much discussion, they clarified their Big Thing: "To eradicate the devastating effects of Lyme disease by 2035 or sooner."

The excitement and energy in the room was palpable, but as the ownership team got clear on the company's Big Thing, an issue that had been negatively impacting the company came to the surface. I reassured the group that when you clarify and commit to your Big Thing, you summon up the thing or things that must change in order to reach your goal.

With this perspective in mind, we dove in. For several years, there were important promises among the owners that had not been kept. Making matters worse, these broken promises had not been addressed. Because there was no immediate and clear solution, the topic of broken agreements had been avoided. This eroded trust, and because this company had been started by a group of close friends who were willing to do what needed to be done, no one complained. Yet, resentment grew.

I invited the team to face these issues immediately. In response, the ownership team took full responsibility and addressed each broken promise. This obstacle was put on the table for all to see and solve, and eventually the owners worked out new agreements. This ushered in a new era in the company, and most notably inspired an opportunity—creating a new culture of responsibility and accountability moving forward.

This cultural shift led them to make significant changes in

the company structure and staffing. It also led to a major restructuring of their profit model. All these were needed changes that they hadn't been able to see.

In the year following our meeting, Ampcoil doubled in size, sales, and impact.

Don't Let Your "Story" Stop You

There's what occurs in life, then there's your story about it. I can sit with any person, and in less than five minutes, tell you their future. This is possible because a person's future is alive in their language. Most people are unaware that they're speaking about their future today. Your language is forming it all the time, whether you're conscious of it or not.

Language reveals perception. The words are expressing what you perceive to be true.

Imagine that you're a slide projector, and your thoughts form the lens through which you see the slides in the carousel. If you have a thought that says, "Things never go my way," and someone gives you a "slide" of $100, how would you experience that act of generosity? I suspect you might be suspicious, or even waiting for something bad to happen. How might you show up if this is how you saw yourself? Would you ever buy a lottery ticket? Climb a mountain? Start a business?

Now, imagine cleaning the lens of disempowering thought on your projector and replacing it with, "Good things happen to me often." Now, when that person gives you a "slide" of $100, how might you experience it?

You have the ability to clean your lens. You are not at the mercy of your default thinking. Most people have their understanding of cause and effect backward. We are who we *say* we are, and who we *see* ourselves to be. This is our *story*, and we're always free to do a rewrite. Are you seeing yourself as you *are*, or as you *fear* yourself to be?

BELINDA:
FROM GIANT DEBT
TO GIANT ASSET

Belinda had been stuck for several years and came into coaching to remove what she referred to as "the big block." Early in our conversation she mentioned a loan that was "looming over her head." She described this debt as if it were a dark and evil monster, keeping her from her dream. "It's hanging over me and it's pressing down. It is crippling me," she confessed.

She had built a story around this chunk of debt that basically said she could not live her dreams until it was fully repaid. She also believed she was bad for letting it happen in the first place.

I asked how she felt when she thought that story. She said that thinking these thoughts felt like a heavy black ball in her chest, oppressive and cold. She felt depleted and stuck.

"What behavior do you engage in when you feel that way?"

"I don't engage. That's the problem."

She was shutting down, hiding out, and not being proactive. I asked her to consider what her life would look like in five years if she did not shift this pattern. With tears in her eyes, she admitted, "Not a future I want to have."

I had her go back to the black ball of heavy, cold energy in her chest. I encouraged her to feel it and allow it to be there without pushing it away or judging it. I challenged her to simply be with it.

"Feel and observe it," I said. "Now, ask the ball what lesson it's here to teach."

"Perseverance… and forgiveness," she said.

Though the words came out of her mouth, she said she was unclear what they meant.

I suggested she consider that one pathway to greater perseverance might be through forgiveness, but she couldn't see what she needed to forgive.

I asked, "Perhaps you could forgive yourself for the story

you've made up about both the debt, and what it means in your life. You've been telling yourself that this debt is crippling you."

She smiled in recognition.

I asked, "Is it really true that the loan is crippling you?" Slightly defensive, she confirmed it was debilitating.

I pushed a little farther. "Pretend you're a lawyer, and make a case for this loan actually strengthening you."

She reluctantly obliged and was surprised to discover several things. She had taken on the debt to support her ex-husband, but now that they were divorced, she was free to create the life she truly desired. This was something she believed had not been possible in her marriage. She also acknowledged that having this loan made her stay at her old job longer than she wanted, which actually supported her in generating a very large book of business and relationships that would go with her to a new position. Finally, she realized that having this loan sparked a resolve to get back on her game and be successful again.

Now she saw some possibilities for a new story about the debt. Belinda realized she had been lying to herself for nearly ten years. She was not limited or crippled. She was, in fact, *strengthened* by this loan. She could not see it before because of her story about it. However, her new shift in perception cut something free. She felt a rush of inspiration and energy. She now saw numerous possibilities to grow her business. We began drawing up a plan for her to skyrocket the business over the next year.

With tears in her eyes, she said she felt as if a hundred pounds had been lifted from her shoulders. The weight had been lifted, and she had done it herself. She left the office on fire and with a plan.

Over the next twelve months she not only doubled her business, she radically increased her confidence. More than get her groove back, she initiated a new future that was significantly elevated in both joy and results.

Pain is Inevitable. Suffering is Optional

Life is not without its challenges. Pain cannot be avoided, but there's a clear distinction between pain and suffering. Pain is the sensation of discomfort, sometimes extreme. Pain can be emotional or physical. However, suffering results from the story we create *about* the pain, and what the pain means to us, to our life and to our future. While pain may be inevitable, suffering is optional. Consider this: suffering will keep you in the pain longer. The story you make up about the discomfort will determine your experience. In some cases, this can be the difference between life and death.

JULIE:
HOW CHANGING HER STORY
SAVED HER LIFE.

Julie sought coaching to assist her in clarifying her Big Thing. She shared that she had been struggling with bipolar disorder for many years which, at times, manifested as debilitating depression. After so many years, she had developed various self-care and coping skills to help her deal with these dark periods. Often, she even managed to function normally through them. Nevertheless, in her mind, it felt like her condition presented a barrier that, in the end, would be impossible to overcome.

As we got to know each other, we began the journey of exploring her Big Thing, but before we could get very far, Julie was diagnosed with Stage 4 lung cancer. The doctors said it had been in her body undetected for some time and had already metastasized. She was terrified. "This shouldn't be happening. This is devastating. What am I going to do?"

We talked through her shock and fear about the diagnosis, then we explored what she might be making it mean. This was a delicate matter because it's no joke when you're talking about someone's very life. While she didn't have complete control over the disease, she *did* have control over the meaning she gave it. Eventually I asked, "What if this diagnosis is actually an opportunity, not a curse. What if you chose to see it as a gift?"

"How in the world could this be a gift? They're telling me I'm going to die."

I gently persisted. "But if we look back in ten years and realized that it *was* a gift… what *might* the gift be?"

She widened her eyes and said, "Well, perhaps I would stop focusing so much attention on my past and my resentments. Maybe it would actually help me to let go of my frustration and judgment regarding the bipolar disorder. Maybe, by surviving this, it will show me how strong I am and that, even though I have my challenges, I'm actually very much alive, and have a lot to contribute toward helping others."

The energy in the room sparked with a palpable hint of possibility. I asked her how she felt.

"Energized, alive, clear, at peace." She said she was experiencing a shift, perhaps an epiphany. She felt lighter. She genuinely believed that more was possible despite her struggles and the daunting diagnosis. It was a feeling that came from deep within.

Then she blurted, "This is God's little gift." She continued, "I'm choosing to believe this is a gift from heaven, specifically for me, that will help me become the person I want to be and do what I was born to do."

Julie replaced the word "cancer" with the term, "God's little gift," and she never said the C-word again.

By shifting her story about what the situation meant, Julie became resolute that she was not ready to leave this earth. She had more to do. Even though she had doubts, she was now determined to break through this challenge so she could stay on the path of her Big Thing. It inspired new actions and direction.

Our work took an important turn that was focused on who she needed to become to release the cancer and create optimum health. She became bold in her caring for herself and went to great lengths to make sure she had the very best care. She spent time visualizing herself in great health. She switched doctors and followed her instincts as well as her medical team's guidance.

She also sought alternative practices and visited special clinics to radically change her diet. As her health began to slowly improve, she demonstrated her decision to go on with her life as normal, and the identity of a dying cancer patient was put completely out of the realm of possibility.

In one of our conversations several months later, she said that the depression had completely lifted. "Before, I was focused on the past and my fear of the future. I scared myself half to death with my thinking and was, at times, like a prisoner in my own house. Changing the meaning I gave to the situation put me in a new mindset. I'm now focused on creating my life, living fully, and doing what I came here to do. Now, thanks to 'God's little gift,' I'm inspired, and being the woman I've longed to be."

Thankfully, three years later, she was in remission. The tumors were completely gone and just a few lesions remained in her bones, and they were stable. She shared her experience with friends, acquaintances, and others struggling with depression, bipolar disorder, and other health issues. Her journey continues to be an inspiration to many.

Changing her story about the diagnosis altered the way she approached her entire life. She was no longer controlled by bipolar disorder. She focused on her health and living fully, rather than her illness. She became inspired and vibrant, key factors in staying alive.

Most importantly, she has become a brighter, more committed, and bolder version of her true self. Julie turned this challenge into an opportunity to free the person she truly was deep inside.

The challenges you face on the road to your Big Thing are very often the blocks you've been carrying but have simply not noticed. By moving toward your Big Thing, you will summon forth whatever's been holding you back. This is not a problem or a reason to turn back. It's a great opportunity to release that block for good. In this way, you use the challenge to let go of extra weight in your pack.

CHAPTER 8

Use It All to Serve

SERVING ROLO PULLS
ME OUT OF SUFFERING

Day 8
Jan 28, 2011 • Aconcagua High Camp 2
Nido de Cóndores • 18,208 feet

It's a rare moment when the weather is clear and still. We're taking a rest day. The sky is intense azure blue, like I've never seen before. It arches to the horizon, hundreds of miles away. Its electric color pops in contrast to the snow that blankets the cliff we're standing on. Our four orange-and-grey tents hug the granite wall as we stand in awe of the many shades of red below. I'm eating tuna from a foil pouch with a cracker. My head feels like it's about to explode, and food is the last thing on my mind. I'm not hungry, but know I need to eat. The team looks on with concern. Out of sorts, helpless and emotional, I delicately take a seat on a boulder. Everyone is tired and not their normal chipper selves.

I've spent the last few hours in the tent simply breathing, trying to feel the discomfort, and hoping to God it would let up. It didn't. The good news was that I was no longer making up any stories about it. I plainly ask Mike, our head guide, "Does this constant pain mean I'm in danger? Am I going to die?" We all had a laugh at that, but I was serious.

"The pain may not go away, but you don't yet have cerebral edema. Your body is adjusting and doing what it was designed to do."

"OK Mike, I'll keep climbing until you tell me it's not safe to continue."

Desperate to feel better, I search my mind for something to take the edge off, or better yet, replenish depleted energy. I don't know what to do. I feel the audible rumble in my belly. There's an awkward silence.

Suddenly, a question rises within. I'm surprised it comes up because of how horrible I feel.

I blurt to the whole group, "Hey guys! What's your Big Thing?"

Blank stares.

Troy asks, "The Big Thing? What's that?"

These words had never come out of my mouth before. I played them back in my own mind, and chills ran up my spine. I continued, "What's your dream? You, know, that thing you know you want to do but maybe you've never spoken it out loud. I'm talking about the most important goal of your life at this time. The thing that, if you don't do it, will have you feel like you avoided the real reason for coming into this life. *That* thing."

Eyes squint. Foreheads wrinkle. A few confide they don't really know. However, everyone eventually attempts to artic-ulate their answer. I'm beginning to feel some vitality again, the headache is less debilitating. It feels good to take the focus off the discomfort. Eyes start to sparkle and laughter begins to emerge. I'm feeling more energy, more life. I smile for the first time in days, and the team is quick to point that out.

When we reach the last guy in the circle, Vince repeats the question. "Rolo, what's your Big Thing?"

Rolo, one of our assistant guides, gets very quiet. His eyes get watery. A moment passes before he speaks. In a thick Argen-tinean accent, he says, "I always dream of climb Denali."

Denali, also called Mt. McKinley, is the tallest mountain in North America, at 20,310 feet, and is located in Alaska. It is the third-highest of the Seven Summits.

Rolo begins to share the reasons why he would never be

able to do it, the least of which is finances. For him, that mountain was beyond his mental reach. He couldn't even fathom a world in which he could actually do it. We see his pain in believing it's impossible. He admits that he's resigned to never do it, yet it's clear that this was his Big Thing.

Guys are wiping tears away as he pours his heart out. Then a miracle happens. A unanimous and instantaneous response arises from our team: "We're going to help you do your Big Thing." I pull out my journal, and we sketch out a plan with Rolo. More tears, but this time with bursts of laughter, and a lot of high fives.

Contribution as a Motivator

Whenever you need a boost, helping another is the fastest way to feel better. This conversation with Rolo and the group woke me up. It stoked deep feelings of aliveness. This is the power of service, an important element of The Big Thing Effect.

It can be small, but serving others will lift you. It will give you energy. We've all heard the phrase, "When you want something, give it away." That day at Camp 2, I gave energy to Rolo. The whole team did. This changed the vibe for the rest of the climb. It gave me a boost that helped to keep going and, as it turns out, it was a turning point in Rolo's life as well. It helped me feel a sense of purpose greater than my own desire to climb Aconcagua. It also had me realize that even though I was in pain, I still had something to give.

Serving engages the universal desire to make a difference. We will get out of bed for others on days when we might not get out of bed for ourselves. This also helps us to not be so egocentric and self-absorbed. (Everyone's a little self-absorbed. It's in our genes.) Focusing on service helps you connect to your heart and gives in-depth perspective on what you might do that is not solely about you.

Gamechangers don't curse their circumstances. They take what they're given and use it to serve.

AMANDA:
TURNING HER STRUGGLES INTO SERVICE

When I met Amanda, an interior designer and real estate developer, she was at what she called, "the low point in her life." After years of struggling with emotional trauma, Amanda was now recovering from painful back injuries that required multiple surgeries. She eventually spent fifteen weeks in a treatment facility for severe depression, compounded by a debilitating endocrine disorder.

In our early meetings, Amanda's focus was on her health. When I asked what she wanted to create, given all she was facing, her response was incredible. "I want to use everything I'm going through to help others persevere. I want to help eradicate the terrible stigma of mental health issues in American society. I want to turn my pain into purpose and help others who are struggling."

I could see her tenacious spirit, even at such a painful time in her journey. She had no idea how she would actually do this. Many would have said it was pointless to aspire to such a lofty intention when she was struggling day-to-day with her own well-being.

Yet, it was that Big Thing—and her deep desire to use it to serve others—that motivated her. This helped her on days when she fought to help herself. She thought about others in pain. It fueled her fire. She intended for her Big Thing to help the world, even though she wasn't sure how, or even *if*, it was possible.

Amanda said this larger intention to use her challenge to serve others was the catalyst that helped her recover. She saw a bigger picture for her life. Even though she had moments of doubt, she stuck with it.

Today, seven years later, she has helped to raise an astonishing $60 million dollars for a new non-profit that will provide mental health treatment to anyone who needs it in Colorado. This non-profit will also work to de-stigmatize mental health.

She did this all while building another nonprofit organization called *Girl Power* that empowers girls to reach their full potential. They provide education, mentorship, and outdoor programs to help girls thrive mentally, emotionally, and physically. This organization has become a shining light of hope for many girls throughout Colorado.

Amanda didn't stop there. She's now embarking on a capital campaign to raise another $100 million to build a comprehensive treatment facility, the first of its kind in Colorado, that works with both behavioral and mental health issues. She's been a vocal advocate for people with mental health challenges by standing up and sharing her challenges. Thanks to The Big Thing Effect, this has also elevated her business. *Luxe,* and other prestigious magazines, are now featuring her work.

Serve Yourself First

Did you know that plants don't grow in the daylight? They collect and store the energy from sun during the day, and then, at night, they use that energy to grow. If there was only daylight, the plants would be stunted. This is why vegetation struggles to bear fruit in the polar regions, because, in summer, the day extends nearly twenty-four hours. The quiet, dark, and restful night is actually when the garden grows.

The same is true for us. During the day, we're taking in so much stimulus and doing so much activity, but most of our restorative metabolism occurs in the quiet of sleep. If you're spread too thin, not getting enough rest, you'll actually keep yourself from growing. Your growth depends on you prioritizing self-care. Doing so allows you to make an even greater impact.

You can't serve others well if you're not serving yourself first. You can't give from an empty vessel. Seeing to your mental, emotional, physical, and spiritual wellbeing gives you needed capacity to serve. Self-care is not a luxury. If you don't fill yourself up from the inside, your days will become heavy and bleak.

Growing up in rural Nebraska, the ethos was "work hard."

While this is a healthy lifestyle, there always seemed to be more work! It never stopped. My family prided ourselves on working from sunup 'til sundown, with little time for play or rest. While as a kid I did get to play sports, I grieved for my parents who were stuck in what seemed to me an indentured life. What was it all for?

Many of us have mastered caring for others. We care for our spouses, partners, friends, pets, children, employees, colleagues, parents, and even Airbnb guests. But are you caring for yourself? I'm not talking about self-absorption. I'm talking about self-care. Many judge this as selfish. The same people find themselves resenting those they serve and succumb to burnout.

I've noticed some people resist going for their Big Thing because they fear it will pull them into an unhealthy balance of overwork. While this is a legitimate concern, I'm not suggesting you run yourself ragged. Rather, if you're going for your Big Thing, you must build a robust practice of self-care. That's not being fanciful—it's just common sense.

BYOB: Be Your Own Bestie

There's another form of self-care that's important and life changing. It's your relationship with yourself. It doesn't matter how intelligent you are, or how successful you may be. If you're relating to yourself in a critical, impatient, uncaring way, you will not draw forth your greatest potential. More notably, you will certainly not experience the deep fulfillment that life has to offer.

"I can only have as good a relationship with another as I have with myself."

When I was in college, I went home to visit my parents and they grilled me about the girl I was dating at the time (not Lindsay) who they had met on previous visits. In a caring way, they confronted me about how she was treating me. From their perspective, this girl was critical and did not appreciate me. Being parents, they were naturally concerned. They strongly encouraged me to give her feedback about how she treated me, and if she didn't change, to break up. I understood what they were saying, but I struggled to address it with her. I stayed in the relationship, and it only got worse. My parents grew increasingly resentful of her, but I was the one who allowed her behavior.

The reason I allowed her negative behavior was because I was embroiled in a negative relationship with myself. I was judgmental and hyper-critical, incessantly focused on what was wrong with me, and then beat myself up about it. I was impatient and expected perfection.

No one knew this was going on inside, because, with other people, I was the opposite. I treated others well, and no one suspected that I was treating myself horribly.

We often focus on how others treat us, without examining how we're treating ourselves. Right now, as you're reading this, you're engaged in a real-time relationship with yourself. This relationship is defined by the way you interact with, think about, speak to, and treat yourself. Are you a caring, patient, and encouraging friend? Or are you a harsh, critical, unforgiving troll? If you're like I was, you treat yourself worse than anyone you've known. Worse yet, we're often unaware it's even happening. What's surprising and also sad is that most of us tolerate this self-abuse. If anyone treated you as harshly as you treat yourself, you'd un-friend them on Facebook and block them on Twitter.

PAT:
BEING A CHAMPION WON'T MATTER
IF YOU DON'T SEE YOURSELF AS ONE

I've worked with several world champion athletes, but one of these clients didn't feel like a champion on the inside, despite being an icon. He's one of the best of all time, with multiple world titles. From all appearances, he had it all: wealth, fame, and world domination in the sport he loved. In one of our early sessions, we diagramed his relationship with himself. He confessed to being highly judgmental of himself and also extremely harsh and impatient. I was aware of his athletic prowess (the whole world was) so it all began to make perfect sense. He was so unreasonably critical and demanding of himself that he became one of the world's most flawless athletes. The unrelenting demands he made of himself had positive external consequences.

This is why so many of us are not willing to release our death-grip on this self-abusive behavior. It serves a purpose, but there's a very dark side, and that's our inner mental climate. You cannot sustain a harmful relationship with yourself for very long. It's only a matter of time before it catches up with you. This client was no exception. His abusive relationship to self had beaten him down. He was depressed and his dark night of the soul spanned a decade.

The conversation exploring his relationship with self quickly cut to the heart of the matter. These dynamics were playing out in other relationships as well. Taking an honest assessment of how he was being with himself, and then shifting it, has resulted in significant breakthroughs for him, including seeing the end of long-suffered panic attacks, and coming to feel like the champion he actually is.

Exercise:
Relationship with Self

Relationship with Self
Imagine your "Relationship with Self" as a scale like the diagram on the next page.

Where do you fall on this continuum?

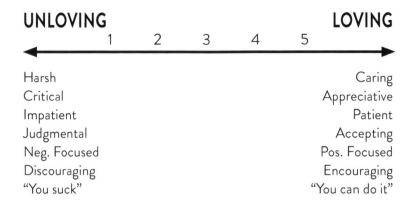

UNLOVING   **LOVING**

1   2   3   4   5

Harsh	Caring
Critical	Appreciative
Impatient	Patient
Judgmental	Accepting
Neg. Focused	Pos. Focused
Discouraging	Encouraging
"You suck"	"You can do it"

If you look at the continuum, from unloving to loving, how are you relating with yourself? Are you hypercritical, impatient, and constantly beating yourself up? Or are you an encouraging friend who sees the best in you? On a scale of one to five, where would you place yourself? Perhaps you're somewhere in-between.

Reference the key below:
1. Unloving. Impatient, demanding perfection from yourself. Harsh and critical. Your self-talk is focused on what seems to be wrong. You feel beaten down and tired.
2. Sometimes loving, occasionally patient. You expect perfection from yourself but know you can't be perfect all the time. You're kind on rare occasions, but still mostly harsh with yourself.
3. Occasionally loving. You are beginning to engage in caring self-talk. You're not mean, but still doubt yourself. You're beginning to catch yourself in negative self-talk, and exhibiting more patience.
4. You focus 50% on what's good. When you catch yourself being critical, you shift your focus toward what you're doing well, and what you can appreciate. Your self-talk is slightly more supportive than it is destructive. You are intentionally being a caring friend to yourself.

5. You're consistently kind, patient and encouraging with yourself. You regularly feel appreciated, and it's not dependent on feedback from others. Your self-talk is often encouraging. You consistently feel inspired.

Wherever you are on this scale, it's my hope that illuminating this will assist you in breaking through to a healthier relationship with yourself. Take these steps:

- First, honestly assess where you are on this scale. Put an X on the diagram where you would rate your current relationship with yourself, 1 to 5.
- Then, write down a description of what that looks like, specifically. (Use the key on the previous page to guide you.)
- Next, circle the number that represents where you would like your relationship to be.
- Then, write out a description of what that looks like. For example, you might say, "I'm consistently taking time to accept myself as I am and appreciate what I bring to life. I catch myself in negative self-talk more quickly than ever before. When fear creeps in, I shift my attention toward what I want. I find one thing to celebrate daily. I'm encouraging myself through positive self-talk every day."
- Review the description of how you do want to relate to yourself consistently.
- Take one small action daily that is aligned with this new way of relating to yourself and watch what happens. Notice any slight shift toward greater self-love, and celebrate it.

When you shift your relationship with yourself, it will immediately impact your energetic state. This naturally affects your relationships with others. For example, if you start being more supportive of yourself, you'll feel energized. It's very likely you'll then naturally bring that encouragement to others.

Also, you'll be more receptive to others' encouragement. When you exhibit the behaviors you *want* from others, then you'll notice that behavior will also *come* from them. If you wish to be treated with more respect, start respecting yourself. When you begin shifting this self-relationship, you naturally level-up who you're being. It lightens your load. It's one of the most powerful acts of self-care.

Allow Others to Serve You

Asking for assistance and allowing others to support you is another meaningful form of self-care. Your Big Thing, by definition, cannot be done by you alone. Getting help will elevate both you and your Big Thing.

GETTING HELP TRANSFORMED ME AND MY BIG THING

In the spring of 2005, I was still living in Los Angeles taking whatever acting work I could find. I worked nights at a swanky restaurant and did production work during the day to make ends meet. Although I booked regular acting gigs, I couldn't create enough consistency to get ahead. I lived in a 400-square foot apartment, and by "apartment" I actually mean "room." I was broke, in debt, and washed the dishes in the bathtub. I had been in this rut for nearly five years. I felt ashamed. For someone with such potential, I should have been so much farther along. This couldn't be my life! I was dead tired and wondering if I'd ever wake up from this nightmare. When I looked at my bathtub, each dirty dish represented a dream unrealized. (On the upside, I could shower and do the dishes at the same time.)

You know that feeling where something feels off, but you don't know what to do about it? I didn't know what I needed to do, but I knew I needed help.

I called my friend Julia, a gifted life coach. After an hour of speaking with her, I felt a glimmer of hope. However, I could not afford her fees. She offered to coach me pro bono for a few months. She was an angel.

I started making a plan to realize a long-held dream of joining the cast on *Saturday Night Live*. Despite my passion, I'd never actually made that my sole focus. Over several months of working with Julia, I shared my hopes and aspirations as an actor and the future I desired to create.

In one of our sessions, Julia reflected something back. "Every time you talk about your future as a successful actor, you invariably end up on a stage, telling people to go for their dreams. You mention very little about the acting and light up when you mention inspiring people."

I agreed. "Well, yes. That's *why* I want to be successful. I ultimately want to help people go for their dreams and live their best lives."

She continued, "Do you believe you *have* to be a famous actor to do that?"

"I never actually considered that... but I think that's what I believe."

"What if you just did *that* instead?"

My mind went numb. I was afraid to let go of my acting career because I'd been chasing it for so long. I believed that the best way to prove my credibility as a motivator was to demonstrate success on the world's largest and most intimidating stage, Hollywood. But acting had lost its luster even though I was still committed to doing whatever it took.

She said, "I have an intuition that you should watch *Contact*," (the 1997 film starring Jodie Foster and Matthew McConaughey). I drove to Blockbuster to rent the video and then home to watch it.

In this film, McConaughey plays Palmer Joss, an author and influencer, who encouraged people to live their best life. As the movie ended, I burst into tears. Up to that point, I would watch McConaughey in films and say, "I want to *be* Matthew McConaughey. I want roles like *that*." However, when I watched *this* film, I realized that I didn't want to be Matthew McConaughey, the *actor*. I wanted to be Palmer Joss, the *character*, the leader, the writer, who helped people see their life from an elevated perspective.

As the credits rolled, so did the past few decades in my mind. It was all starting to make sense. The happiest moments had occurred when I'd been encouraging people to go for their dreams. From my earliest days on the farm to the later days in Hollywood, I often spent up to six hours a day talking with people who called me for advice. I loved helping them find their Big Thing. It was the best entertainment, and sometimes I couldn't help but share ideas, and introduce them to people who might be able to help. My acting career was only impinged by the daily calls and follow up with the many people I spoke with.

I recalled the countless auditions where I would stay after to coach fellow actors in the waiting room to ease their fear, visualize success, and have their best audition. In fact, I'd even taken on four clients at one point in 1999 because they insisted that I coach them. Then, at the Honda dealership, I had created a coaching program for the salespeople, and even encouraged many of my customers to go for their Big Thing. Now, thinking back, there were several people who said, "You should do this... you have a gift."

I thought all the way back to childhood and preaching to the corn. This wasn't just something I wanted to do. It was who *I already was*. I'd been doing it all along. It took getting coached to realize it.

The next morning, I woke to a strange, energizing yet peaceful feeling. I sat up in bed with a calm sensation, as if all was going to be OK. I began imagining myself on a stage. I wasn't acting, but speaking to an audience. I could see myself in jeans, a sport jacket, and sneakers, with one of those mics that goes over the ear. I was sharing success principles punctuated by stories. I also imagined myself coaching one-on-one. I saw clients flying from around the world landing in a quaint, mountain town, where I would coach them in an office that overlooked the ski slopes. As I played out this daydream, I became overwhelmed with excitement. Hollywood was no longer my passion. Something bigger had emerged. I had discovered my new Big Thing.

By the end of 2007, my Los Angeles life had completely shifted. I stopped auditioning and completed a Master's Degree in Spiritual Psychology at the University of Santa Monica. I delved into several years of accelerated coaching training and became a Professional Certified Coach through the International Coaching Federation. I also began teaching classes at the Agape International Spiritual Center with one of my mentors, Rev. Dr. Michael Beckwith.

Use Your Intuition

Intuition is the ability to understand something without analytic reasoning. Many refer to this inner knowing as a "sixth sense." Like the sense of sight, sound, smell, touch or taste, your intuition occurs as a feeling within your body (or mind) that only you can experience. Because this sensation is so personal, no one else can tell you if you're in touch with it or not. Your intuition is a superpower, and everyone has it. The question is, will you listen?

Your path forward is not a one-size-fits-all formula. Your Big Thing has within it the unique steps and insights necessary to help you realize it. Many times, those steps will defy logic and call you to take unexpected turns that your linear mind can't fully understand. Guidance comes from within as well as from outside. Slow down and sense it. If you're distracted and spread too thin, you won't be able to pick up those subtle cues.

Like a treasure map that you must follow, in order to see the way, you must look beyond the obvious clues. Utilizing your intuition will help you to detect the clues that will illuminate the path to your Big Thing.

HOW INTUITION LED ME
WHERE MY MIND COULDN'T

In 2008, after visiting my friend Sonny in Colorado, I realized that this was the direction my Big Thing was leading me. *Maybe I should move there?* It felt so risky. I asked for a sign. Walking through downtown Santa Monica, I noticed a white dove hovering over the hood of a black Mercedes across the street. It was snow white, perfect. I walked closer and watched it. I was overcome with a feeling of complete peace. The dove eventually flew away, and I forgot all about it until two days later.

I was visiting a friend down the coast near Hermosa Beach, about fifteen miles south. I was standing on the balcony telling my friend about potentially moving to Colorado, my arms resting on the railing, when something landed on my shoulder. I craned my neck to look. It was a white dove. It looked at me like a long-lost friend. I was once again overcome with a feeling of warm and soothing peace.

A few days later, on the phone with my Grandma Rubesh, I shared the story of the white dove. Grandma said, "Oh Jeffrey, don't you think that's some sort of omen?" I explained that I had asked for a sign about moving to Colorado. She left our conversation saying, "Honey, how much more of a sign do you need?"

Within thirty days, I took the leap and moved. I built my practice into a handful of great clients, and coached them at my new home on the river. While I was proud of the progress, there was still the weight of massive debt which now included school loans. Although my coaching with Julia had completed some time ago, she encouraged me to reach out to our mutual friend, Stephen McGhee, for coaching. Stephen lived in Denver and we reconnected. Several months later, we were on the top of Grays Peak where he invited me to climb Aconcagua.

When you ask for help, it will find you. Staying in touch with your intuition, honoring it, and acting on it courageously, will help you see it clearly. This is the Big Thing Effect in motion.

Exercise:
Elevate Your State with Service

This five-step exercise will change your state at any time.

1. Set a timer on your phone for one hour.
2. Walk out into your world and serve for the entire hour at your highest level.
3. Look for ways to serve and do it.
4. Be kind, and do this full out, from your heart (with no expectation or need for anything in return).
5. After the hour is up, notice how you feel.

This is very simple, yet can also be challenging. Step out into your world and serve someone. Look for a way to serve at your highest level with no expectation of anything in return. If you live in a remote area, it might be helpful to drive to a location that's more densely populated. I do this exercise often, where I will simply walk and go where my feet lead me and serve anywhere I see possible. My inner focus is to serve at an *absolute 10*. That means giving all I've got to help in any way that's caring and doesn't hurt myself or another. This can look like helping someone with their bags, giving directions, or even picking up a small piece of trash. There's no limit to what this can look like.

Your mind will try to complicate this and may also be concerned with how you'll be perceived. Notice how that feels and keep on with the exercise. You can help others in ways that are obvious. You can also help in a way that's less obvious, such as smiling at a stranger or wishing a blessing upon them.

The only parameter is that you spend the entire hour focused on the act of serving. In the end, if you let go of the mind chatter and give, something beautiful happens. You'll notice that you have something to offer. You'll also feel the vitality that surges when you give at your highest with no expectation of a return.

CHAPTER 9

Let Go of
the Guarantee

CONFIDENCE IS FLIMSY

Day 11
January 31, 2011 • Aconcagua High Camp 3
Plaza Colera • 19,200 feet

We finally reach High Camp, roughly 4,000 feet below the summit. This is the last stop. The wind screams sideways as we struggle to pitch camp in blowing snow. My mind is cloudy. My head still throbs. The weather only heightens the dark abyss of the cliffs and distance we had climbed. Dennis joins me, taking it all in. He looks at me with steely blue eyes and says, "Well m' boy, do you think you're gonna make it?"

I'm not sure if it was the lack of oxygen or Dennis's powerful presence, but the combo sparks an insight. "Whether or not I *think* I will make it is irrelevant." I am shocked to hear these words coming out of my mouth.

For so much of my life, I'd spent hours, more like days, OK, months, stewing on the thought, "Can I make it or not?" and in many of those instances, I stalled out well short of the goal. It was all about confidence in myself. Here, on the edge of the planet, staring across the jagged Andes, I saw the pattern that had snuffed the life out of many of my aspirations. Dennis had catalyzed one of the most significant realizations of my life.

"I can't be certain that I'll make it. The only thing I can be certain about is my commitment."

His surprise at my answer was visible in his eyes, even through his goggles. I had no way of really knowing if I would actually summit. If I developed cerebral edema, I'd have to turn back. There are some things I could do to help prevent that, but ultimately it was not in my control. I couldn't, in full integrity, say, "I will make it to the top." What I *could* say in full integrity was, "I'm *committed* to climbing to the top." *That* I could deliver on.

So, rather than constantly taking the measure of my confidence, how I *felt* about my chances, how much I *believed* in myself, I focused on my commitment and who I had to be to make good on this commitment.

The certainty of commitment was a lifeline. It brought me back to center when the icy winds clawed at my face. Nothing else was certain. There was no other guarantee.

In this manner, I was bringing certainty into the uncertainty. Being certain in my commitment was reassuring, grounding, empowering. When I felt uncertain of the outcome, I rested in the certainty of my commitment.

Certainty in Place of Confidence

Confidence is fragile, while certainty is, well, certain.

Are you asking yourself questions like, "Can I make it?" "Will I make it?" "Do I deserve to make it?"

If so, you know you're in the confidence conflict.

These questions snare you because you could debate them for days. If the answer is, "No, I can't do it" then what? If you're like me, it will piss you off! If your answer is, "Yes, I can," what happens the minute you doubt that thought? The whole line of questioning is disempowering.

Everyone wants to know that their Big Thing is possible, yet no one has a crystal ball guaranteeing that they will win the gold. This is naturally frustrating to the ego. Are you unconsciously searching for a guarantee that doesn't exist? Once you accept that there are no guarantees of the outcome, you can choose to fully commit.

Confidence in an outcome is weak because it's beyond your control. Confidence, by definition, is merely opinion—yours.

It depends on believing you'll reach your goal. If you believe you will, you feel good, but if you believe you won't, you feel bad. It's a Tilt-a-Whirl ride that will leave you nauseous. Stop the nonsense of thinking you need to believe you can do what you're setting out to do. Belief is not a prerequisite. In fact, many well-intended people try to work up their level of belief, like froth on a latte, but ultimately this is wasted energy.

A commitment is simply a decision: "I am choosing to do this thing." When you decide to do something, you cut off all other options. This is a choice, not a question. Instead of living into the question, "Can I make it?" live into the decision, "I *choose* to make it." Let this be the stance you come from and let your action rise from this position. More than where you're going, commitment is about where you're coming from.

You must shift from the question, "Can I?" to the declaration "I *choose*," and then live into that choice. That's a commitment. You can be certain of your ability to choose. You can't be certain of whether or not you'll reach it. However, in my experience, when you live into the choice to reach it, you most often do! The rare times when you haven't reached the intended outcome, there's a gift in the result.

This process can feel messy, and it's scary to the ego. The Old You is holding on for dear life, trying to convince you that you can't change, and won't get there. But this is a *delay tactic* to back you off the edge and away from your Big Thing. If you *do* back off, your ego has won. This is where most people tap out.

Tapping Out

There's no shame in turning around on any adventure. There will be times in life when turning back is the smartest thing to do. It's OK to turn around. Just be sure you're turning around from a place of clarity, rather than fear.

When this happens, and it happens to everyone on a Big Thing, ask yourself *which part of you is wanting to turn around, the old you or the new you?* When you do that, remember that you don't have to make the decision alone. Your teammates—your supporters—want to help you. Let them.

I recall asking Mike just above basecamp if it was safe for me to keep climbing. I said, "Mike, I'm so far past my comfort zone, I can't tell if this pain is telling me to suck it up or pack it in." Mike had seen it all in his fifteen years guiding on the mountain. After prefacing that only I could make the decision, he assured me that it was safe to continue, provided we keep a close eye on the symptoms. If it weren't for his support, and I was left with only my normal way of operating, I would have retreated days ago.

At some point during your Big Thing, you'll be tempted to turn around. Because every Big Thing has a "Windy Traverse," where you come face-to-face with your own monster, whether it's fear, doubt, discomfort, or your old way of being. It's a natural milestone on your journey, the "All is Lost" moment, and it always attacks when you're close to reaching the summit. It doesn't mean you're on the wrong mountain. You haven't made a wrong turn. Retreat may be an option, but know you are close. Lean on your team and ask for help. You don't have to go it alone. In fact, that's the beauty of a team. What you can't do alone, you can do together.

CHAPTER 10

"Die Trying"

CONTINUE OR RETREAT?

Day 12
Summit Day • The Windy Traverse
Mt. Aconcagua • 21,290 feet

Frozen. No ropes, no oxygen, no one to turn to. I can't stop staring at the German climber, his red suit is barely visible through the blowing snow.

I'm in shock. *Oh no. This can't be happening again.* I'm having flashbacks of the body bag dangling from the helicopter on Longs Peak.

The panic of that moment is piling on top of this one, and I can't stop thinking that it *was* a premonition after all. *You're gonna die on this mountain!*

I'm alone with my inner voice. *Are you out of your mind? This is clearly a sign to turn back. What are you thinking?* I crave clarity but find none. The rest of the team is 1,000 feet above. *What do I do? What's the right decision? Continue or retreat?*

Rolo, who had been climbing behind me, is suddenly by my side, talking to basecamp on his satellite phone. He turns to me and yells over the wind, "I must go down... Maybe miracle... Maybe alive!"

I stare back in shock. Everything feels like it's happening in a dream. "Of course," I yell back.

"I put you with new team before I go. They coming right behind us."

I nod without thinking.

We wait until the other team approaches. Rolo knows the guide, and they talk in a language I don't understand, the sounds garbled between the weather, my hat and down hood.

"You go with them, OK? I catch up."

I nod again, unsure if I want to continue, but there isn't much time to think. If I am going to go, it has to be now because the new team is continuing to climb.

Rolo retreats and begins his descent, and I join the back of the group as we continue across the traverse.

I climb on for a little while, but, as daylight is dwindling, so is my confidence. I stop for a moment, look back over the edge, and see Rolo kneeling next to the German climber. He puts his hand on the man's chest and looks up. He sees me looking down and shakes his head. No miracle.

It's all too much. Mentally, that puts me over the edge. I turn around, stumble a few steps downhill, and fall to my knees. The fog in my brain settles into darkness and my eyes are heavy. I feel like I'm starting to lose consciousness and all sense of time. I let my eyes close for a moment. I tell myself that if I can just take a short rest, yes, I'll be OK.

Suddenly, I hear a thumping sound. It's Rolo. He's slapping my face. He screams, "No sleep! Must keep climb!"

Gasping, I lean heavily on my ice axe as Rolo lifts me to my feet. My knees buckle again.

The wind, the cold, and the altitude gang up against me, and I'm absolutely lost. I struggle to make a decision, but I can't. Like my fingers, my will is frozen.

I soon realize, the mountain is not the monster I need to defeat. The monster is the old way of being, Needy Man. He's fighting to stop me, breathing fire, seeding doubt in my mind. *What if you make the wrong choice?*

I scan my reflection in Rolo's goggles. I realize there is no right choice here. There's no guarantee. There's only the choice I'm willing to commit to. My conversation with Dennis yesterday comes back to mind.

I was sick and tired of turning around when things got

stormy. The thought of giving up was suddenly more frightening than death. This time, whether I made it or not, I was going all the way with my commitment.

I will NOT die on this mountain. There's more to do. There's more to be. There's more to give. Wiping ice from my goggles, I gaze up toward the summit and ask, "Who do I have to *be* in this moment to reach the summit? What would *Miracle Man* do?"

The answer was not what I expected.

"Breathe."

So, I do that. I lean against the granite wall, rest and breathe.

Rolo places a hand on my shoulder, and we stand there for maybe a minute or two, or ten. I fight for each breath and begin to recite the old mantra, "One breath at a time and everything's fine." I'm breathing and repeating this over and over. I slow everything down to this single moment, just like I had done on Longs Peak. I begin to feel the sensations in my body. The pangs of fear, the throbbing in my hands, the pressure from the altitude in my head. All of it.

I decide that I need to stop trying to catch up to the team and stop judging myself; I need to make peace with my pace. I repeat, "One step at a time and everything's fine."

I turn to Rolo, "Let's go."

He grips my shoulders, turns me around, and together, we take a step, then another. I focus on my breath and continue to repeat my mantra.

Left foot.

Breathe.

Right foot.

Breathe.

Together, we inch across the rest of the Windy Traverse and on to the final ascent. I grunt with each step up the ridgeline, determined and present.

It was the longest three hours of my life.

With the summit in view, I grasp the granite outcrop with my left hand while using my ice axe to pull myself up the last few feet.

At 2:33 p.m. on Feb 1, 2011, I take the final steps, putting my boots on the top of Mt. Aconcagua with Rolo by my side.

Within moments, I fall flat on my back next to the shiny aluminum cross that stands three feet high and signifies the highest point in the Western Hemisphere.

I'm spent, exhausted, and struggling to breathe. After a few minutes, oxygen returns to my body, and tears fill my eyes. There's nothing in any direction but clear blue sky. At 22,841 feet, the sun seems so close I could squeeze it like a Nerf ball. And the headache is gone. Thousands of feet below, snowstorms and clouds blanket the Andes. For fifteen minutes, I'm above it all and take it all in. I hear the voice of Mike, our head guide, ringing in my mind. A bit of wisdom he had offered days earlier at basecamp now came alive with profound meaning. "The summit is for the ego; the climb is for the soul."

I replay in my mind what I'd been through: the intense fear and doubt, the pain I'd endured, and all the training over the last nine months. But the real breakthrough is the realization of who I'd *become*. I'd wanted to give up so many times that I thought it was a sign I wasn't meant for such a feat. I felt like a coward during most of this journey, the old identity demanding I back down and leave well enough alone.

The obstacles that normally turned me around became opportunities that strengthened me and revealed qualities I had not experienced so fully before. I wasn't impervious to fear, nor free from questions and doubts, but I had summoned strength from within when I needed it most. I had turned back, surrendered, and lost consciousness at one point, then, thanks to Rolo, found the depth of will to continue. I had exchanged confidence for commitment. I was a changed man.

The old Jeff died on the Windy Traverse. A new man stood on the summit. He was different. He was changed.

He was radically alive.

CHAPTER 11

The Return

LIKE A BAT OUT OF HELL

Day 14
February 3, 2011 • Basecamp
Plaza Argentina • Mt. Aconcagua • 15,290 feet

I slip out of the tent at 4:30 a.m. and sit on a canvas chair under the stars. It's warm, 30 degrees Fahrenheit, and completely quiet. My left thumb and big toes are still numb from summit day, just two days ago. Last night we pitched camp here at Plaza Argentina, one of two basecamps here on Aconcagua. We celebrated late into the night, swapping stories with other climbers, drinking Red Stripe beer and listening to Reggae. Today we'll hike from basecamp back down to the hotel at Los Penitentes.

The South summit of Aconcagua stands high above, cloaked in dark shadows. Dawn breaks and bathes the East face in a palette of pewter and amber. It's such a massive presence that I can feel the tug of its gravity. Now, somehow it feels comforting and grounding. Perhaps that's why I slept soundly last night sandwiched between Stephen and Dennis. Apparently, they jabbed my ribs through the night in hopes of stopping my snoring. It was the best night's sleep in ten years.

My body is rested, my mind is energized and ready for the double marathon hike down to the park entrance. After breaking camp, we prepare for our descent. Mike encourages us to start slow because 26 miles is longer than you think. We heeded his advice but the farther we got, the faster we went.

The walk became a saunter; the saunter a trot. Soon, we were stallions running wild down a dusty riverbed.

After three hours, we stopped to hydrate. The river rushed powder blue with glacial melt, and there's a sparkle in everyone's eyes. I looked back at the summit, another planet hanging in the distance. No words were spoken, but backpacks were slowly put back on, laces tightened, and everyone smiled. Mike warned, "Guys I'm serious. Careful of the pace!"

In less than ten minutes we were back in a sprint, with Dennis leading the way. My feet were on fire, but it was nothing compared to the past fourteen days. Three hours later, at the trailhead, we were high-fiving and hugging. We piled into the white van with no seats. The driver handed each of us a Red Stripe and said, "Hold on."

We fish-tailed out of the park toward Los Penitentes, laughing and joking and pinching ourselves to make sure we were actually off the mountain. Fifteen dusty minutes later we arrived at the hotel where we had checked in 15 days ago. Getting out of the van wasn't easy. My body was so tight that I could barely stand. We hung outside of the lobby waiting for another team from Canada who was checking in.

Their eyes were wide with anticipation. The leader was fidgeting with his wallet, pulling out his credit card. He seemed concerned as he watched us just outside the glass door. A feeling came over me and as he paid for their rooms. I approached him. I must have looked a wreck because his eyes widened with concern. I flashed back to the swollen face of the Swedish climber and his dire warning.

With tears in my eyes, I put a hand on his shoulder and said, "This mountain changed my life. Enjoy every moment."

Coming Home

Pursuing your Big Thing will transform you. It will draw greatness from your depths like nothing else. You will shift first on the inside, and then, through challenges, those shifts will integrate and become part of you. Then the outside will begin to change. When you reach the top of *your* mountain, it's essential to remember that you must also get back down.

Returning to your previous life, you'll take this newfound growth and strength with you. In the months that followed my return from Aconcagua, more insights began to emerge. I noticed things I hadn't seen before.

I saw my girlfriend Lindsay in a new light. I noticed how desperate I had been for a guarantee in our relationship. The pain inflicted by my parents' divorce clouded my view of marriage. I wanted to know I wouldn't be hurt and that it would last forever.

The epiphany on the mountain that Dennis inspired helped me to see that I couldn't control the future with Lindsay. In matters of love there are no guarantees, but the real element missing was my commitment. I couldn't *guarantee* we would live happily ever after, but I could be certain of my *commitment* to love her with all my heart, and to remove anything in me that might get in the way. A healthy and happy future was possible, even if it wasn't guaranteed.

One afternoon, hiking along the Roaring Fork River in Glenwood Springs with my dog, Bailey, I was wrestling with the question, "Is Lindsay the one for me?" And wouldn't you know it... walking on the trail not ten feet in front of us was a white dove, and Bailey didn't even bark. Two months later, I proposed, and we've been happily married ever since.

After the climb, the team and I became devoted to supporting Rolo, our climbing guide, in fulfilling his Big Thing, climbing Denali.

To fundraise for him, we produced and hosted a Leadership Conference at Red Rocks Amphitheater in Denver, where we led the audience through a day of leadership training. We also led all 100 participants through one of our team workouts! To bolster the fundraising for Rolo, I created and facilitated several Leadership Hut Trips deep in the Rockies near Aspen. All proceeds went to the "Rolo Denali" Fund. Collectively, our team raised the $24,000 necessary for Rolo's climb, and we arranged all the logistics.

On May 24, 2013, accompanied by fellow teammates Mike Bradley and Vince Ruland, Rolo made it to the summit of Denali. Rolo says it changed his life forever.

No Holding Back

Providing the spark for Rolo's Big Thing, and helping him to succeed, changed my life forever. It gave me the inspiration and determination to hold nothing back in the way I serve clients in their Big Thing. No more waiting to feel ready or discounting my experience. Before the expedition, I was stuck in Small Vision Syndrome, waiting for that special someday when I felt confident enough to go that big. The only thing that kept that from me previously was the old "Needy Man" way of being. Now "Miracle Man" created each day with a sense of urgency and purpose. Now I let go and went wild with service. I would no longer wait to make a difference. I had transformed confidence into certainty.

This new way of being started producing big results. Over the next year, my business doubled. The work was no longer about the need for others' approval. It was about serving and making the world a brighter place filled with people committed to their Big Thing.

Another surprise was realizing a long-held dream of owning a home on a gold-medal trout river, where Lindsay and I would raise a healthy, happy family. In the pursuit of my Big Thing, and my intention to serve others, I had taken my focus off building a dream home. After several years of applying these principles, I turned around and there it was, another example of The Big Thing Effect. As I write this, I'm staring out the window of my office in Aspen overlooking the ski slopes. It's a long way from doing dishes in the bathtub.

CHAPTER 12

Are You Ready for the Climb of Your Life?

ARE YOU READY FOR
THE CLIMB OF YOUR LIFE?

You made it! You've followed me to the top of the world and back. I appreciate your guts, your heart, and your willingness to come this far. You could have put this book aside hours ago, but you didn't. That speaks volumes. It means you must have a Big Thing pulling at you.

Now, it's your turn. Don't merely chalk this up to an inspiring conversation—food for thought, good information. I asked you at the beginning: What would you dare to do or "die" trying? What's your Big Thing? I hope that you've become clearer on your answer to this question. Most of all, I hope by now you're inspired to go back through the chapters and do the exercises, move through the journey for yourself, and take on the climb of your life to your own mountaintop. An adventure that will inspire you to take the risk and feel more radically alive than you've ever known awaits. Just making the commitment to clarify your Big Thing will set the Big Thing Effect in motion.

This is your moment to shed the fears of the past, the old habits that left you second-guessing, and any remnants of Small Vision Syndrome. Use the endeavor of your *Big Thing* to ignite the person you've always intended.

Imagine how you'll feel. Consider what your life will look like.

I urge you not to put it off by saying, "next week… next month … next year." We all act like we have all the time in the world, but none of us knows how long we have. If not now, then when?"

You are more than your circumstances, more than your past, more than the "you" you've believed yourself to be. You came here to unlock the power of the one-and-only *real* you.

If you have doubts or feel fear, remember you are not alone. I am right here with you. Lean on me as your guide, because, like my Dad said, "I don't *think* you can do it. I *know* you can."

The moment is here. You've heard the call. Your Big Thing is waiting.

ACKNOWLEDGMENTS

To my beautiful and amazing wife Lindsay, and our girls, Emory and Brooklyn. You are the sun that lights my sky. I'd like to thank my parents, Al and LeeAnn Patterson, and Dale and Bev Rubesh—for your love, example, and guidance. Stephen McGhee, thank you for the incredible experience climbing Aconcagua, and your invaluable coaching and friendship. Thanks to the rest of the members of our team: Troy Wagner, Dennis Carruth, Vince Ruland, Eric Wiseman, Greg Aden, and our guides, Mike Bradley, Rolo Abaca, and Augusto Ortega. I want to thank my clients for their amazing presence and for letting me share their stories. To Orvel Ray Wilson, whose coaching and support made this book possible. To Julia Nadine Padawer for your support all these years and your input on this book. A special thank you to Susan Suffes for the editing and encouragement. To Alyssa Ohnmacht for your perfect timing and layout of the book. Finally, to a few of the mentors I've had the pleasure of learning from: Drs. Ron and Mary Hulnick, Rev. Dr. Michael Beckwith, Steve Chandler, Ray Miller, Cheri Helmer, Roger Harpham, Pat Felix Brauer, Coach Charlie Thorell, and Coach Jim Komenda.

ABOUT THE AUTHOR

Jeff Patterson, M.A., P.C.C., coaches innovators who are committed to changing the world and leaving a legacy. Known for his keen instincts and ability to cut to the heart of complex matters, Jeff helps clients elevate their vision of what's possible, increase their impact and overthrow the tyranny of limiting patterns that keep people playing small.

A certified professional coach, he holds a Masters of Spiritual Psychology from the University of Santa Monica. Jeff lives with his wife Lindsay and their two daughters, Emory and Brooklyn, in the mountains of Colorado. When he's not fly-fishing in his backyard, you can find him inspiring audiences around the world.

To arrange for Jeff to speak to your company or group, email info@TheBigThingEffect.com.

A SPECIAL INVITATION

If you're ready to apply The Big Thing Effect to your life or business, I'd love to hear from you. Email: info@ TheBigThingEffect.com

Check out the website www.TheBigThingEffect.com for many free resources to assist you on this journey, and to engage The Big Thing Effect community.

– Jeff Patterson

Made in the USA
Monee, IL
31 January 2023

26238408R00122